HOW TO WRITE SHORT STORIES

ARCO

HOW TO
WRITE

Short
Stories

Sharon Sorenson

MACMILLAN • USA

CONTENTS

Part 1

Getting Started

CHAPTER ONE
Defining and Characterizing the Short Story

A short story is a narrative. It tells about imaginary events that happen to imaginary people, and the events lead to a crisis which is resolved at the end. As an imaginative literary form, the short story varies from author to author.

DEFINING THE SHORT STORY

Master story writer Edgar Allan Poe said that a short story has a beginning, middle, and end. In the beginning the characters meet, in the middle they face growing conflict, and in the end they resolve the conflict. By taking readers from the beginning through the middle to the end, the author conveys a message, or theme.

Learning to develop the art form includes two steps, one simple, the other a lifelong effort. First, you must learn the elements of the form: plot, character, setting, and theme. That is the easy part. Second, you must practice combining those elements until your skills are as finely honed as those of Poe or O. Henry. That is the lifelong part.

EXAMINING THE GENERAL CHARACTERISTICS

The short story includes certain general characteristics. Although the approach to and interaction with these characteristics is the stuff by which short stories vary, certain elementary techniques will help a beginning writer develop a story. A short story, in general, should

—develop believable characters with whom readers can identify, and characters whose motives readers can understand,

—develop a plot that includes conflict, rising action, climax, and resolution,

—have a setting consistent with the characters' personalities,

—contain a theme, or message, for readers,

—follow a consistent point of view,

—use dialogue appropriate for the characters,

—show, not tell, about characters, themes, and conflicts through concise, specific description,

—include imaginative language, imagery, and literary devices (such as flashback, symbolism, and foreshadowing),

—maintain a consistent tone and mood,

—be of appropriate length, from 200 to 10,000 words, but most likely 1500 to 3500 words,

—result in a single effect, so that every character, every action, every word leads to the single effect.

Developing the short story takes careful thought and planning, but not every writer works the same way. Some writers begin with a message, an idea they want to share with readers. Other writers begin with plot and create characters who can develop the plot and thus generate a message. Still others begin with characters, let them interact, and allow the plot to develop from the interaction. Most writers, however, follow a kind of "yo-yo" process, changing characters as the plot develops and altering scenes to improve characterization. No matter which process serves you best, you must reach a certain point in the prewriting stage before you can begin to put words on paper. At that point, you should be able to put the specifics in this three-part sentence:

1. My characters will interact in these ways . . .
2. in order to achieve this resolution . . .
3. so that readers will get this message.

In order to arrive at that point, you must thoroughly prepare. This book strives to help you with that preparation and then to take you through the steps to completion.

The following model short story will serve as the basis for discussion in future chapters. Read and study it now. Look for the general characteristics of a short story.

STUDYING A MODEL SHORT STORY

MOSQUITO
by David Ciepley

"They're not landing on me."

"That's 'cause you used too much bug spray," whispered Brian.

"But I washed it off," replied Andrew, who started to raise his arm to his nose for a double check.

"Shhh!" hissed Todd, his older brother.

The tent crossbar, and the flashlight suspended from it, rocked gently in the night breeze, swinging the dirty cone of light first toward Andrew, then around in a loop to catch the tight faces of Brian and Todd, and then again to Andrew's before re-settling in the middle, bright upon their bare, extended arms.

SLAP!

"What'd you do that for!" Todd demanded without lifting his eyes.

"It was hurting," said Andrew, as he carefully picked the mosquito from the small stain in which its crumpled body adhered. He flung the thing to the ground in sudden aversion and wiped his arm on his pant leg.

"You're a chicken-liver," said Todd.

Todd had been watching one for over a minute now. First there's the tiny prick, and then nothing, as the flow of anesthetic does its work. Then the flow reverses, bringing the dish-shaped cells and their broth one by one up the proboscis and into the mosquito's gut.

"I've almost got one," Todd announced as he sidled his opposite hand from his elbow back towards his shoulder, where the mosquito slowly swelled, sanguine. A quick pinch of the surrounding skin, and a sudden rush of blood inflated the mosquito's belly before it could pull away. The pressure was too great, and the mosquito burst in a splash of red.

"Cool!" yelled Brian.

"Gross!" yelled Andrew.

The sly smile which always announced his intentions of mischief worked into the corner of Todd's lips, and with a sudden lunge, he was across the tent bearing his shoulder down on Andrew, who in compromise, threw up his sleeved arm to spare his cheek.

"Quit it!"

The two older boys giggled, Todd beaming as he retreated.

"Let's tell ghost stories," Brian suggested.

"I don't like ghost stories," said Andrew, wiping his sleeve off on his other pant leg.

"Why not?" pushed Todd.

"I just don't."

"It's 'cause you're a baby and a mamma's boy."

"Shut up!" Andrew spat out the unfamiliar shape of the word.

"Don't you ever tell me to shut up!" Todd menaced.

"Let's play Truth or Dare," Brian broke in.

"Okay," replied Todd, as if it were the original suggestion.

Andrew didn't like Truth or Dare either, but this time he remained silent.

"Truth or Dare?" Todd demanded at him.

"Why me first?"

" 'Cause you're the youngest. Truth or Dare?"

"I don't wanna play."

"You gotta play, or we'll send you back to the house."

"That's not fair," whined Andrew, but he gave in.

His brother, Todd, was a Dare person, but Andrew always chose Truth. He still smarted from revealing his secret love for Julia, the blue-eyed girl who moved to their farming town from California; it was all over school the next day. But the thought of jumping off roofs and eating spiders caused greater nauseation.

"Hurry up! You always choose Truth anyway."

Andrew was instant in opposition.

"Dare!"

Brian and Todd, already mulling over painful little truths to squeeze out of him, were caught naked. Recovering, they edged to the corner of the tent, and in whispers interspersed with dry laughter, worked out an appropriate rebuff. Soon afterward, they confronted Andrew, Todd the spokesman.

"Go into the woods and fill this cup with water from the creek," adding in afterthought, "and you can't take your flashlight."

They handed him an orange-juice stained cup and awaited his reaction.

Andrew thought of the creek in the woods at the opposite end of the field. It wasn't that far—a hundred yards to the first line of trees and only thirty or forty into the woods. He liked walking along the stream in the early spring, when morning light filtered through the naked trees. But after sundown, the woods transformed.

"That's not fair. It has to be inside the tent."

"Of course it does not," replied Todd, with a convoluted certitude that killed the objection.

After a pause, Andrew explained. "It's dark. . . ."

"Yeah, it usually *is* at night. And that's why you still sleep with the covers over your head—'cause you're a baby and you're afraid of the dark."

"I am not."

"Then go get the water."

Andrew hated this. It wasn't so bad when it was just he and his brother. But now Todd had to show off, and Andrew, wanting so much to be accepted, had to suck it up.

"I'm gonna tell."

"Fine. See you in the morning."

Andrew flung aside the flap and stomped out. But he wasn't going to go back to the house. That was admitting defeat, and next time, his mom wouldn't let him come because he couldn't get along.

The moon was half in shadow, only dimly illuminating the field. Up ahead, the stretch of trees blended vaguely with the ground, so that far off to the left and right, differentiation became difficult. The line seemed to shift in the breeze.

This was the upper end of the farming belt. North of here, the forest stretched solid, fading from hardwood into pine once it reached Canada. He had been told this was Sasquatch country, home to those prehistoric men-animals that roamed alone or in small bands, occasionally coming out from the eaves of the forest to wander through an outlying farm. Mr. Warten, from a farm down the road, told a story about a Sasquatch who came snooping near his chicken coop and sent the chickens into a frenzy, waking up the whole household. It rained later that night, but he said that in the morning, he could still see the indentations from where its monstrous feet had cut across the field.

Andrew started to jog across the field, deciding that, in any case, it would be better to get in and out quickly before anyone, or anything, could spot him in the open. He stumbled often, for the field was deeply furrowed where, in preparation for planting winter wheat, the razor-disks had sliced it open and the plow had turned it over. Half way across the field, his foot caught on some stubble, and he went sprawling onto the moist earth. He lay there for some minutes, on the verge of tears, wishing he were home. He thought of turning around and going back, past the tent, to their house beyond the swell, but he discarded the idea as he had before. Then he thought he might urinate in the cup, for his present dilemma had well-prepared him for the function, but he knew he could never pass if off as stream water—they would smell its peculiar salty bitterness. He worked himself to his knees, stood up, and without brushing off, continued his jog to the forest.

He didn't pause once he reached its eaves. Scrambling over fallen logs and darting between leaning trunks, he kept on going, fearing that if he stopped, the sounds of the forest would keep him from starting again.

He quickly reached the stream and peered over its crumbly, vertical bank to the trickling creek four feet below. Putting his back to the creek, he felt his way down the bank, waving his foot across its face until it hit a sturdy root on which he could ease his weight and send his other foot out to search another hold. At the bottom, he scooped his cup through the muddy water and scrambled out.

The woods seemed unnaturally quiet now. Perhaps his noise had silenced the forest voices, but perhaps something else had. He could see the flitting brightness of the moon-lit field from between the tree trunks, and he made a path straight for it. He had just stumbled on a stump which sprang up at his feet when, off to his left and a little behind, a sharp movement in the bush announced another presence.

On a level track, a professional sprinter can run a hundred yards in under ten seconds. Across the plowed field, Andrew wouldn't have been far behind. He crashed through the tent flap, his lungs heaving, his cup down to a half-inch of worm-infested mud, and his animal smile slashing at the faces of the older boys, whose card game his violent entry had upset.

He grimaced at Todd.

"Truth or Dare?!" He could already picture Todd gagging as he tried to force down the slimy mud to uphold his forthcoming end of the bargain.

Again, that sly smile brushed Todd's face as he read through his brother's excitement.

"Truth," he replied.

ANALYZING THE MODEL SHORT STORY

The short story above includes the general characteristics listed at the beginning of this chapter. Note the following:

—Readers can identify with the characters in this story. They are believable kids, throwing insults and dares at one another, the older boys hoping the younger "mamma's boy" will "go tell" and be forced to stay in the house for the rest of the night. The story says "kids will be kids." You will read more about creating characters in Chapter Three.

—The plot includes several kinds of conflict, both external (between the brothers) and internal (the younger brother's struggle with himself), as well as struggle with the environment (at least in the younger brother's imagination). Rising action, climax, and resolution, discussed in Chapter Four, are readily evident in the plot.

—The setting is consistent with the characters' personalities, especially since the "camp out" is in the family's backyard. You will examine setting more carefully in Chapter Five.

—The message for readers is clear: learning to deal with older children's taunting is part of growing up. For young readers, the message is one of supporting counsel; for mature readers, it is one of memories—fond or otherwise. Chapter Two discusses theme in short story writing.

—The writer tells the story from the omniscient point of view, but readers learn most about the younger brother's point of view. For example, when Andrew chooses Dare, readers learn that the older boys "were caught naked." But readers also know how Andrew feels about being sent to the woods. Only the all-knowing, all-seeing point of view permits the author that privilege. Chapter Six includes more about establishing point of view.

—The early dialogue helps readers identify the characters and their relationships to each other. Dialogue also establishes much of the early plot. In short, the dialogue gives readers their best clues about the characters. Chapter Seven includes all the rules about writing dialogue.

—Concise, specific description shows, rather than tells. Readers are not told where the story takes place; rather, they see the inside of a tent and learn later that the tent is near the house, near a field, near the woods. Readers are not told that the older boys are out to taunt Andrew; rather, they see example after example of Todd physically and mentally shoving Andrew into frustration. Readers are not told how Andrew's fears grow; rather, they see him stumbling across the field in the dark and "hear" him thinking about Sasquatch. Writing good description is the topic of Chapter Eight.

—The story includes vivid imagery through the many sensory details: blood bursting from the mosquito, the circle of light in the tent, the smell of urine, the sounds of fear in the night. Certain literary devices appear. For instance, the symbolic mosquito helps readers identify the significance of the story's title. You will learn about imagery and literary devices in Chapter Eight.

—The story's tone and mood are consistent with plot and character. The tone and mood help readers identify with Andrew, his fears, his struggle to be part of the crowd. Chapter Eight will also help you learn how to establish consistent tone and mood in your own short story.

—A relatively short version of a short story, the model fits the general length requirement.

—Every character, every action, every word leads to the single effect.

Future chapters will refer to this model short story. You may need to reread all or portions of it as you continue working with the prewriting stages and as you study specifically about theme, characters, plot, setting, point of view, dialogue, and description.

CHAPTER TWO
Determining the Theme

Before you can plan specific incidents in the story line, you must know your purpose. In general, short stories are written to entertain, but specifically they evoke certain feelings—like fear, joy, grief, amusement. In the model short story "Mosquito," for instance, the writer evokes memories of childhood relationships between siblings, relationships that were painful at the time but are only a twinge in the memories of mature readers.

DEFINING THEME

Closely related to purpose is the message you hope to convey. That message is called the story's theme. It is like what children call "the moral of the story," but the theme is not always a neatly stated moral. Of course, the theme can be stated, but it is most often implied. Usually this message is an insight into life or human nature.

CONVEYING THEME

How do writers convey their themes? They do it by putting characters in conflict with one another. What happens as a result of that conflict reveals the writers' message. For instance, think about "Mosquito." The writer puts two brothers in conflict with one another in the presence of the older brother's friend. The pressure to "show off" for the friend creates a series of conflicts which finally result in the younger brother accepting—and carrying out—a dare. As a result of that conflict, readers learn that surviving taunts from older children is part of the struggle of growing up. Younger children have to fight to overcome the image of "mamma's baby." The theme is a simple one.

Now, if the characters had been young adults facing conflict in the corporate office rather than in a backyard tent, the writer may have been saying that the "initiation" into the world at large is an ongoing struggle with superiors who want to see if the employees "measure up." Thus, as characters and conflict change, so the theme changes.

HINT:

The theme is closely related to the outcome of the conflict.

FINDING A THEME

So, what do you hope to say to your readers? Too early to know, you say? No! If you have no message, you have no story. You cannot reach your destination without a sense of direction.

How do writers decide on a theme? The answer, of course, varies from writer to writer, but consider these possibilities for your own short story:

—Have you witnessed some event that made an impact on you? Maybe a tornado hit your town. Or a friend was jilted. Your little neighbor girl's puppy was killed. You were dealt a bad deal when you bought a used car. Or you were involved in or witnessed some kind of accident.

—Are you frustrated by social concerns over which you seem to have no control? Are you familiar with specific instances? Such as waste in government spending? Unfair laws which let the victim suffer more than the criminal? Or welfare benefits going to the undeserving? Men being paid more than women to do the same job?

—Do you find yourself struggling with personal dilemmas? Like being torn between responsibilities at work and at home? Or feeling wretched about being unkind to a good friend? Or trying to accept rejection at home or on the job? Or facing the death of a friend or family member? Or dealing with success in spite of jealousy from others?

All of these general situations offer the promise of a specific theme for a short story. For instance, assume a tornado hit your town. You saw neighbors helping one another who in the past had hardly spoken. Because you witnessed tragedy bringing people together, you may want to write a short story about that experience. Your plot may actually include the tornado, or it may address some other tragedy that allows you to bring characters together. But you will probably never *say* in your short story, "Tragedy brings people together." Rather, through your characters, readers will come to understand your message, your theme.

Consider other examples. Perhaps you are frustrated by social concerns over which you seem to have no control. Your short story may share that message with readers by recreating a specific situation in which the frustration surfaces. Your short story tells the tale of a victim of crime and lets the reader see the victim's agony and the apparent lack of justice. You never *say* the situation is unjust; through your character, readers experience the injustice for themselves.

Or you have just caught a friend lying. That inner jolt may be the basis for a short story about two friends who face a crisis, reject one another, supposedly resolve their differences, but never resume the old really close friendship. By writing a story about these two friends, you convey your message that lying creates distrust.

POSSIBLE PITFALL:

Avoid tackling a broad, complicated plot in a short story. Keep in mind that theme is *broad*, but your short story is a *specific* example of the theme.

Stop now and write a sentence which expresses the message you hope to leave with your readers. Consider these examples:

—Living by one's principles requires sacrifice.

—A winning attitude helps people move up the business ladder.

—Winning isn't important; it's how you play the game.

—Treat the land with respect and you will reap the rewards.

CHAPTER THREE
Creating Characters

Believable, motivated characters make or break a story. If readers cannot understand or accept them, nothing else you do matters. Why? The actions of your characters convey your theme.

LOOKING AT CHARACTERIZATION

Two kinds of characters people a short story: major characters and minor characters. Sometimes major characters are called "round" characters because the reader sees them fully developed. The minor characters, appropriately called "flat" characters, have little or no personality. In the model short story "Mosquito," Andrew, the major character, is most fully developed. Brian, the visiting friend, is no more than a shadow. His presence serves simply as an impetus for Todd's desire to flaunt his age.

HINT:

Good characterization, in part, establishes for the reader the relationships among characters.

POSSIBLE PITFALL:

Physical descriptions are not as important as personality traits. Short story writers must create characters quickly; one clear, dominant impression is most important.

Before you begin writing your short story, then, develop a character sketch of each of your characters. Writing the sketches will help you focus on dominant characteristics, and by directing your full attention to characterization at this point, you can avoid problems later with inconsistent or improbable portrayals.

Use the following steps to choose appropriate characters for your short story and to create a character sketch of each.

FINDING SUITABLE CHARACTERS

Fiction writers find characters for their short stories all around them. Certainly fictional characters, by their definition, come from the writer's imagination; but often real people provide the stimulus. Consider the following sources:

    people at work
    people at your family reunion
    people who live on your block
    people in your sorority/fraternity
    people in your club
    people on your athletic team

When you have a list of a dozen or so people, think about each. What characteristics do these people have that will help you create effective characters that in turn will aid in developing your message? Like many writers, you will probably blend characteristics from several people to generate your fictional character.

CREATING CHARACTER IDENTITY

Working with only one character at a time, answer the following questions about your main characters:

—What are the characters' identities? Names? Ages? Nationalities?

—What do the characters look like?

—What is their background? Family? Education? Business experience? Home life? Hobbies?

—Put your characters in a setting. What kinds of things do they like? Plush furniture? Luxury apartment? Bare walls? Rustic cabin? Disheveled office? Open water? Northern forest?

—What do your characters think about? How do they react emotionally to frustrating situations? How do they react to success or embarrassment? What is important in their lives?

—How do they behave, move, respond?

—What do your characters sound like when they talk? What kind of vocabulary do they use? Is it consistent with other aspects of their personality?

—How do others react to your characters, to what they say and do? Do others see them the same way? Do the characters see themselves the way others see them? Who are their friends? Their enemies?

—What are their most unusual characteristics?

POSSIBLE PITFALL:

Avoid stereotypes. Readers find no suspense if they know exactly how a character will behave.

—How do your characters see life differently from most other people you know?

—How are these people different from most others like them?

—What would someone who meets your characters for the first time be most likely to notice—or least likely to notice?

POSSIBLE PITFALL:

Maintaining consistent characterization will be almost impossible if you do not "know" your characters well. You must understand them far beyond the context of the story—both past and future.

By answering these questions, you clarify your characters in your own mind. If as a writer you have a clear image of them, you will better be able to convey that image to your readers.

BEGINNING THE CHARACTER SKETCH

When you have answered these questions, begin the character sketch. Remember that the purpose of the sketch is simply to focus your attention as a writer on the personality traits of each of your characters. You will not include all of the above information in a sketch. Rather, you will most likely include the following kinds of ideas:

—a single focus on the character,

—details about the character that help readers understand the focus,

—character actions that help readers understand the focus,

—character conversations that help readers understand the focus,

—direct or indirect descriptions of the character.

DETERMINING THE FOCUS

When you have chosen your main characters, determine the focus of your sketch of each. List all the characteristics that make each character interesting or unusual. For one character, you may have a list something like this:

called "world's oldest hippie"
considers self a medical healer
invents "contraptions"
built own house
eats strange herbs and plants
makes violins
raises own food—garden, goats, bees
usually looks dirty

From your list, select one idea on which you think you can build a character sketch. Put that idea in a sentence. Note that the one idea may include more than one item on your list. For instance, "considers self a medical healer" in the list above may include eating the strange herbs and plants and raising his own food. All three may, in fact, define "world's oldest hippie." The following example illustrates a single focus on which a writer can base a character sketch:

EXAMPLE:

My neighbor, whom we call "the world's oldest hippie," considers himself a healer, using strange herbs and plants, all of which he raises himself.

In a single sentence, write the one idea on which you think you can build your character sketch. This one idea, or focus, will be important in the development of your short story.

SHOWING YOUR READER

The most important part of portraying effective characterization is showing, not telling, about your subject. Ask yourself at every sentence, "Am I telling, or am I showing?" If you tell readers that "Richard loved children," then readers must simply take your word for it. Instead, *show* readers that Richard loved children. Write something like this:

Richard always met the neighborhood children at the bus stop. Even at 72 he was spry enough to bat balls, throw frisbees, or play a short game of basketball. But when he met us at the bus, he always had some new trick to show us—a wooden top that would spin for long minutes without toppling, a wooden doll-like creature that would climb a pair of ropes, a wooden man that turned flips. Always wooden. Carved and sanded and assembled in his cluttered little shop. And then he gave them away to whoever seemed to show the greatest fascination with the trick of the day.

Not once does the writer say that Richard loved the children, but readers know.

Select one situation in which you can best *show* your character to readers.

CHOOSING A MEANS OF CHARACTERIZING

You can show, rather than tell about, a character by using one or a combination of three means. Consider these options, any or all of them:

Description

To help readers see and know the character, describe any significant features about him or her or the surroundings in which readers see your character. Indirect description can be more effective than direct description. Remember, even in the course of describing, to show, rather than tell. (See also Chapter Eight.)

EXAMPLE:

Weak, telling: He was sloppy.
Better, showing: He dragged his sleeve through the spaghetti sauce.

Action

Rather than tell readers about the character, show the character in action. Remember that by watching their behavior, readers can learn about your characters.

EXAMPLE:

Weak, telling: She was glad to see me.
Better, showing: When she saw me, she ran, arms open, to give me that wonderful bear-hug hello.

Conversation

Let your character talk. Use the kinds of words and sentence structure in the dialogue as you "hear" the character using. You will, of course, enclose the dialogue or monologue in quotation marks. (See Chapter Seven.)

EXAMPLE:

Weak, telling: Jeremy seemed nervous.
Better, showing: "No. I'm okay. Don't bother." Jeremy's tight voice left
                    me unconvinced. "It's just. . . . Well, no, I'm okay.
                    Really." He studied his fingernails.

HINT:

To put it as concisely as possible, a reader learns about
characters by

1. what they say,
2. what they do, and
3. what others say about them.

CHECKING FOR CONTENT

When you have completed your first draft, consider the following
questions as you reread to spot possible weaknesses:

—Does my character become real to the readers?

—Have I made him or her sound special rather than stereotypical?

—Have I maintained a single focus, rather than rambling about all
kinds of interesting but irrelevant details?

—Do all details—descriptions, actions, conversations—support the
single focus?

—Are the details logically organized?

—Do readers hear and see the character?

—Does the dialogue accurately reflect the character?

—Since actions speak louder than words, do readers see the character in action?

—Have I been subtle with details, rather than blunt and bold?

—Do I show, rather than tell, what the character is like?

Any questions to which you cannot answer an honest "yes" may
suggest areas which need revision.

WARNING:

Your character will probably change in the course of the story. Be sure
your reader sees adequate motivation for these changes. Characters are
motivated by

—their ambitions,

—their emotions,

—events in their lives.

The motivation and change must show a clear cause-effect relationship in order for your readers to find the story plausible.

EXAMINING A MODEL

Now examine the following sample character sketch. It employs most of the characteristics listed above. As you read, watch for "showing" words and phrases.

MR. BIDDLEMAN

"Come into the kitchen with me. I'm eating just now." A hint of British accent added a musical quality to his old-man voice. "Let me get you some tea."

A fine old bone-china plate sat on the painted wooden table piled high with books and junk mail.

Whatever was on the plate—unrecognizable by local standards—smelled like a wild combination of garlic and sage.

"Shove the books over; I've your tea here." He placed on the table a cup and saucer that matched the plate. On another saucer were two brownish cookies or thin cakes. "I must say it's so great to see you, my boy. What brings you around to my humble abode?" A glance around the room emphasized humble, but not poor.

Books tumbled over one another on every sitting place but one, the ladder-back rocker in the corner by the window.

"Just visiting. What are you reading lately?"

"Most recently I've been reading up a bit on the ancient herbal medicines. You know the Incas. . . ."

Listening to the details of his past day's reading helped put the room in perspective. The plants on the windowsill, the aroma from the oven, the cookie-cakes on the table, the food on his plate, the trays of dried leaves on the refrigerator, the strings of dried flowers and pods hanging from the ceiling light, the bags of dried grains in the corner, and the fresh vegetable cuttings in the sink wove their way into his recounting of his latest reading.

"It's all in what you eat, you know. Eat up." The cookie-cake things grew uglier by the minute. He wiped his plate clean with some kind of dark brown bread, stuffed the hunk in his mouth, and wiped the dribble from his chin. "Eat up, my boy, eat up!"

Only when the door slapped shut on squeaky hinges after his final goodbye did the overwhelming sensory bombardment drift away with the air. Ah, fresh air.

ANALYZING THE MODEL

The preceding character sketch achieves a description of a peculiar neighbor without *telling* the reader that he is peculiar. Note how:

—The writer shows the eccentricities by allowing readers to see a series of seemingly incongruous characteristics:

- The man uses fine bone china but eats in clutter on an old painted table.

- His speech and the abundance of books "tumbling on every sitting place" suggest an educated man with an eccentric lifestyle.

- Readers see the kitchen, full of herbs living, drying, and dried, and make the connection with the old man's reading.

- Although readers do not know for sure, they suspect the old man may have only recently become fascinated by the effect of certain herbs on one's physical and/or mental being.

- The visitor, obviously unprepared for the experience, finds the situation a bit more than he can bear.

- The writer *shows* that the visitor is eager to leave, *shows* that the old man's conversation causes the boy's mind to wander, *shows* that the cookie-cakes are unappetizing. A good characterization, you will recall, shows; it does not tell.

—The methods of development obviously include all three mentioned above—description, action, and conversation:

- Readers witness the descriptions, see the room, the clutter, the details. They see books, a ladder-back rocker, foods, china, painted table, refrigerator, sink, etc. All aid in characterizing the eccentric old man.

- Readers see the old man in action, not just what he's doing during the visit, but also what he's been doing prior to the visit.

- Readers hear his voice, his words, his accent.

—The mechanics of writing this particular characterization call for accurate use of quotation marks and accurate paragraphing to indicate change of speaker. Inaccuracies here will confuse the reader and cause the characterization to fail.

CHECKING YOUR CHARACTER SKETCH

When you finish your own character sketches, ask yourself:

—Do my characters portray consistent, realistic behavior? For instance, do their reactions grow naturally from their backgrounds?

—Do their surroundings support their values? If not, do I have logical motives for seemingly uncharacteristic behavior? Will my readers accept those motives? Or do I need to alter the characters' personalities?

By working through the questions in this chapter and by creating the character sketches, you will have forced yourself to examine each character carefully, thus working toward consistent, believable characters.

CHAPTER FOUR
Developing the Plot

Once you have selected a message, you must decide what conflict
your characters will face in order for you to convey that message to your
readers. Since you will probably not *state* the message in the story, your
characters and the conflicts they encounter will *reveal* the message.

DEFINING CONFLICT

The conflict begins when the protagonist (main character) faces an
obstacle. Characters may face either or both of these conflicts:

—Internal conflict: conflict within him- or herself. For instance, the
character may wrestle with guilt, sorrow, frustration, depression,
indecision, or inadequacies.

—External conflict: conflict with an outside force. The outside force
may be either the environment (like drought, freezing tempera-
tures, floods, storms, or fire) or another person (like a boss, rel-
ative, neighbor, friend, colleague, or political adversary), called
the antagonist.

DEFINING PLOT

What happens as a result of the main conflict is called the plot. The
plot develops as the protagonist struggles with a problem, finds a solu-
tion, and accepts the changes which result. The parts of the plot
include the exposition, opening incident, rising action, climax, falling
action, and resolution. The following chart defines each of these parts.

PARTS OF THE PLOT

Exposition	Introduces the characters and setting
	Establishes the point of view
	Gives background information
Opening	Leads the main character to a conflict
Incident	Begins the plot

Rising	Builds the conflict
Action	Adds new, more complicated incidents
	Leads to the climax
Climax	Raises conflict to greatest intensity
	Changes the course of events or the way the reader understands the story
	May be either an event or an insight
Falling	Reduces conflict
Action	Prepares reader for the resolution
(not always used)	
Resolution	Ends the conflict
	Leaves the reader satisfied

DEVELOPING A PLOT OUTLINE

Before you begin your short story, you should make a plot outline. Start by answering these questions:

—What event or events lead the main character to a conflict?

—What initial conflict does he or she encounter?

—Is the conflict internal or external?

—Which character is right and which character is wrong or mistaken? Does that change during the story?

—What are the results of the initial conflict?

—How does this initial conflict build to additional, more complicated conflicts?

—What finally brings the conflict to its greatest intensity, to a kind of "boiling point"?

—What is the climax?

—What happens as a result of the climax?

—What is the end result? Does the main character make a major change? If so, what makes him or her change? Is the change a result of a personal realization? Or is it the influence of other characters? In other words, what is the resolution?

As you answer these questions, you will outline the plot of your short story. To help you make all these questions—and your answers—more clear, examine the following model plot outline.

HINT:

Some writers start with the climax and write the plot to fit.

EXAMINING A SAMPLE PLOT OUTLINE

In Chapter One you read a model short story titled "Mosquito." Think about the parts of plot in that story. (You may need to reread all or portions of it in order to analyze clearly.) As you examine the model, compare the full story with the following plot outline. Then you will be ready to write your own plot outline.

A. Exposition
   1. Introduces three characters, Andrew and older brother Todd and his friend Brian.
   2. Shows setting inside tent at night.
   3. Gives background by showing the three boys at a game which requires strong nerves.
B. Opening Incident
   1. Younger brother slaps mosquito because it hurts.
   2. Older brother reprimands him.
C. Rising Action
   1. Older brother calls Andrew "chicken-liver."
   2. Todd allows mosquito to bite.
   3. Andrew shows fear by not wanting to tell ghost stories.
   4. Andrew reluctantly agrees to play Truth or Dare.
   5. He surprises others by calling "dare."
   6. He accepts the dare.
   7. His fear builds as he crosses the field and thinks about Sasquatch.
   8. He vows not to hesitate and gets the water.
D. Climax
   He hears a sharp movement in the bush announcing "another presence."
E. Falling Action
   1. Andrew crashes through the tent flap.
   2. He asks his brother for "Truth or Dare."
F. Resolution:
   Todd, taking the opposite of his usual track, calls for "Truth," thus ruining Andrew's plan to get back at his brother.

POSSIBLE PITFALL:

Remember, story events should be in chronological order, showing a cause-effect relationship. In other words, one event causes the next which causes the next. Your plot sketch, or outline, should demonstrate that relationship.

USING FLASHBACK

Sometimes writers interrupt chronological organization with a flashback. A flashback reveals something that happened earlier, something out of chronological order. Usually the purpose of a flashback is to reveal information essential to the reader's understanding of a character's motive.

EXAMPLE:

Reality set in for Thomas. This week's jolt was just another in a year-long series. First he lost his bid for the advancement. Then his sales territory was expanded, demanding added hours away from home. In late spring he learned that his only son—his pride and joy—faced life-time agony as a result of juvenile diabetes. And now this latest slap in the face. How long could he endure?

The "latest slap," no matter its severity, would not let readers understand Thomas' frustration. Only through the flashback can readers know what else Thomas has faced.

WARNING:

In a flashback—or anywhere else in the story, for that matter—avoid details that are meaningless to the development of the plot.

USING FORESHADOWING

Writers sometimes use foreshadowing as a device to give readers a sign of something to come. Foreshadowing, more shadow than substance, comes in the form of subtle clues, not direct statements. Its purpose is to create suspense, to keep the readers guessing about what will happen when. Consider this brief passage from the model short story "Mosquito":

He had been told this was Sasquatch country, home to those prehistoric men-animals that roamed alone or in small bands, occasionally coming out from the eaves of the forest to wander through an outlying farm.

This brief reference to Sasquatch foreshadows the line:

. . . off to his left and a little behind, a sharp movement in the bush announced another presence.

The reader is prepared for "another presence" because of the suspense-building foreshadowing at the beginning of Andrew's journey across the open field.

While foreshadowing is not essential to plot, many writers do employ the technique. Most often, however, the use of foreshadowing comes as a result of polishing and refining the plot rather than carefully planning for its occurrence in an initial plot outline.

OUTLINING YOUR OWN PLOT

Use the following plan to develop your own plot outline:

1. Before you begin writing the outline, state the conflict of your story in one sentence. For example, in "Mosquito" the conflict can be stated this way:

   Andrew struggles to be accepted by Todd and Brian as "one of the boys."

2. With the conflict foremost in your mind, establish the climax. In "Mosquito" the climax occurs when the sharp movement in the bush announces "another presence."
3. Now, fill in the elements of the rest of your plot. Refer to the sample outline on page 25 for ideas.

CHAPTER FIVE
Establishing the Setting

By now you probably have a fairly good idea where you want your characters to face their struggles.

DEFINING SETTING

The setting is the time and place, or series of times and places, where protagonist and antagonist meet. Characters and action should interact with the setting. Remember, though, that readers learn about the setting through the eyes of the narrator, so a description of surroundings must come through naturally as the narrator mentions details.

POSSIBLE PITFALL:

Avoid long, detailed physical descriptions of the setting for your short story. Atmosphere is more important than the physical description.

REVEALING SETTING

If the setting plays a key role in the plot, you must give vivid details, always being careful to establish the right atmosphere for the characters and plot. More often, however, a short story writer does not devote descriptive paragraphs to clarifying the setting. Rather, readers learn about setting by inference, through hints. For example, the opening lines of "Mosquito" infer the setting through "tent crossbar and the flashlight suspended from it."

Study the following clues from "Mosquito" to see how the writer reveals only the important elements of setting.

TEXT	INFERENCE
tent crossbar and the flashlight suspended from it	inside tent at night
bare, extended arms with mosquitos	warm weather
send you back to the house	tent situated in backyard
go into the woods . . . water from the creek	woods nearby with creek flowing though it
woods at the opposite end of the field	field separates yard from woods
liked walking along the stream in early spring when morning light filtered through the naked trees	*not* early spring or morning
upper end of farming belt	in northern tier of the U.S.
Sasquatch country	probably the Northwest
farm down the road . . . chicken coop	area of small farms
house beyond the swell	rolling land; house not visible from tent
worm-infested mud	suggests late fall
field deeply furrowed . . . in preparation for planting winter wheat	late fall
caught foot on stubble	left from crop harvested earlier in fall

PICTURING SETTING

Before a writer can imply a clear setting, however, he must know *all* of the details—even details which will never appear in the story. As a result, you should write a complete description of your setting as you see it in your mind's eye. First, jot down some notes by answering the following questions about the setting:

—How does the setting look?

—What sounds can you hear in this setting? What do these sounds tell the reader about the setting?

—How does the setting feel? Is it cold, hot, rainy, muggy, dusty?

—What is the setting's mood? Is it tranquil, depressing, eerie?

—How does it smell? What do the smells tell the reader about the setting?

—What is the time of the setting? Present, past, future? Is time of day important? Is time of year important?

—What is the space? Is it acres, miles, a 20' x 20' room?

—Is there more than one setting? If so, ask the same questions about each.

CHOOSING DETAILS

Even though you can picture in your mind's eye all the details about the setting, not all of these details are important to the reader. Include in your story only the details that further the plot or theme. For instance, the author of "Mosquito" omitted the following details about the setting:

—the shape, size, color, or fabric of the tent

—the size or color of the flashlight

—the shape or size of the nearby house

—the kinds of trees in the woods

—the distance to the nearest neighbor

These details would have done nothing to help readers understand Andrew's problem or its resolution.

POSSIBLE PITFALL:

Sometimes setting is not important; the story events could take place almost anywhere. In that case, omit details of setting and provide only a general impression.

Ask yourself the following questions:

—Is setting important to the plot?

—Is setting important to the characters?

—Is setting important to the theme?

If the answer is "no" to *all three* questions, your short story should have few details about setting.

CHAPTER SIX
Selecting Point of View

Because readers identify with the point of view from which the story is told, how you tell your story will determine its message. The cliché "There are two sides to every story" is accurate only as far as it goes. Actually there are as many "sides" as there are people involved. Even someone outside the conflict will have a perspective from which he or she can relate the details, but his or her perspective will necessarily omit the personal reactions of those actually involved in the conflict. He or she has no way of knowing these reactions.

DEFINING POINT OF VIEW

Point of view is the place from which, or way in which, something is viewed. Semantically, that means that there can be three points of view: my point of view, your point of view, and other people's points of view. Language textbooks refer to these as first-person, second-person, and third-person points of view.

In terms of a short story, the point of view is the perspective from which the story is told. The short story is traditionally written from either first-person or third-person point of vew. (Only rarely is a short story written from second-person point of view.) Within the third-person point of view, however, short-story writers recognize three distinct perspectives: third-person, limited third-person, and ominscient third-person.

The following explanations and examples illustrate each of these perspectives. Your task will be to select the point of view from which you can best tell your story.

EXAMINING POINTS OF VIEW

First-Person Point of View

The first-person point of view uses "I," "me," "my," and "our." It permits the author to tell the story from the point of view of a narrator or of one of the characters in the story, major or minor. Only those feelings, observations, and reactions which that narrator or character experiences can appear in the story. The advantage of first-person point of view, of course, is that it puts readers close to the action.

EXAMPLE:

I stood there contemplating the stack of sales records we had to compile before we could call it quits for the day. I just wanted to go home, be with the kids, watch the ball game.

I hesitated. "Well, Krista," I began, hoping she wouldn't be her usual grouchy self, "what do you want me to do first?"

She frowned. "Why don't you sort the reports by department code?"

She sounded cross. I thought I heard her stomach growl. I guessed she must be hungry.

Third-Person Point of View

Third-person point of view uses "he," "she" "they," "them," and "their" as well as people's names. A narrator tells the story, but he is more removed from the story than if he is using the omniscient point of view. In fact, he tells the story from only one character's point of view, only as that character can observe.

EXAMPLE:

She stood there contemplating the stack of sales records they had to compile before they could call it quits for the day. She just wanted to go home, have a quiet dinner with Tom, and curl up with a good book. She looked at Jerod.

"Lazy rat," she thought, "he doesn't even know how to enter the basic data."

"So what do you want me to do first?" he asked.

Krista thought he sounded almost willing to help. She hesitated, looked at him again, frowning, unsure why he seemed so helpful. "Why don't you sort the reports by department code?" she suggested. Silently she added, "And we'll see if you have any idea what you're doing."

Limited Third-Person Point of View

Similar to third-person point of view, the limited third person uses "he," "she," "they," and "them." The significant difference is that this third-person narrator is *not* part of the story and cannot read any character's mind.

EXAMPLE:

She stood there looking at the stack of sales records they had to compile before they could call it quits for the day. She looked at Jerod. It was not a friendly look.

"So what do you want me to do first?" he asked.

She hesitated, looked at him again, frowning. "Why don't you sort the reports by department code?" she suggested.

Omniscient Third-Person Point of View

The all-knowing, all-seeing point of view is almost always that of the author-narrator. Only the author knows all, sees all, understands all. Only he or she can tell what *each* character thinks, knows, feels.

EXAMPLE:

Jerod and Krista stood contemplating the stack of sales records to be compiled before they could call it quits for the day. Neither wanted to work late; that was understandable. But Jerod liked to ease back and let Krista assume the real burden. He hoped she'd make quick work of it tonight. Little did he know that Krista resented his mere presence.

"Lazy rat," she thought. "He doesn't even know how to enter the basic data." Her stomach growled.

By way of summary, the following chart shows the four major points of view:

POINTS OF VIEW

Name	Character or Narrator	Characteristics	Pronouns
first person	either	speaker part of story, can observe all characters, but reveals feelings and reactions only of self	I, me, my, mine, we, us our(s)
third person	either	story told only as one character can observe	he, him, his, she, her(s), they, them, their(s)

Name	Character or Narrator	Characteristics	Pronouns
limited third person	narrator	narrator not part of story, cannot read any character's mind	he, him, his, she, her(s), they, them, their(s)
omniscient third person	narrator	narrator/author knows all and sees all	he, him, his, she, her(s), they, them, their(s)

CHOOSING POINT OF VIEW

The model short story "Mosquito," is told through the omniscient third-person point of view. As a result, readers know how Andrew feels about being sent to the woods, but they also know that Todd is "caught naked" when Andrew surprises him with the "Dare" response.

Imagine how the theme of "Mosquito" would change if it were rewritten in first-person point of view. What if the story were told by Todd? By Andrew? Obviously the author's message would change drastically. For instance, if the author rewrote the story in first-person point of view with Todd as the narrator, we would probably read about an older brother frustrated by his tag-along younger brother. Todd's attitude toward his younger brother, his thoughts about what he can do to make Andrew suffer, his plan to get rid of Andrew so he and Brian can "camp" alone, and his reactions to Andrew's surprising success would all be part of the exposition. Instead of following Andrew into the woods, readers would stay with Todd and Brian in the tent, listening to their giggles about how they finally got the best of Andrew. The message would become one of how to deal with a younger brother.

POSSIBLE PITFALL:

Be sure to maintain a consistent point of view throughout the story.

In short, then, the point of view will determine what you can and cannot accomplish in a short story. Consider the following four sets of guidelines. Choose the point of view most appropriate for which your short story meets *all* conditions.

USE FIRST-PERSON POINT OF VIEW IF

—readers must know your main character's inner thoughts and feelings in order for the plot to advance.

—your main character is best revealed by your telling the story from his or her vantage point.

—you can best establish the conflict by sharing only your main character's thoughts.

USE THIRD-PERSON POINT OF VIEW IF

—using the first-person point of view prevents your showing the main character's weaknesses.

—your message will be more clear with a narrator, slightly removed from the scene, reporting your main character's thoughts and actions.

—the objectivity of a narrator will add strength to either the character or your message.

—you can best establish the conflict by sharing only your main character's thoughts.

USE LIMITED THIRD-PERSON POINT OF VIEW IF

—using the first-person point of view prevents your showing the main character's weaknesses.

—the character is best revealed by permitting readers to observe only what your character does and says.

—suspense builds most effectively because an objective narrator reports what happens.

—your main character's actions are more important than his or her thoughts.

USE OMNISCIENT THIRD-PERSON POINT OF VIEW IF

—readers must know your main character's inner thoughts or feelings in order for the plot to advance.

—using the first-person point of view will prevent your showing the main character's weaknesses.

—your message is most effective when readers learn how all characters feel.

—you can best further the plot by showing all characters' thoughts.

These guidelines should help you think through your own needs. Select the point of view which will best allow you to tell your story, reveal your characters, or otherwise convey your message.

Part 2

Putting It on Paper

CHAPTER SEVEN
Writing Dialogue

You have a plot line; you have characters; you have put them in a setting; you have selected a point of view. Now you are ready to begin writing. As you write, direct your attention to dialogue.

STUDYING THE PURPOSES

Dialogue is conversation. The conversation may be characters talking to each other or may be characters talking to themselves (interior monologue). Dialogue serves two purposes: revealing character and developing plot.

Short stories depend on dialogue to stir the readers' imaginations and promote their understanding of character. A character's spoken words give life to his or her personality. Politicians, for instance, win or lose elections based on their spoken word. Teachers and pastors make their points via the spoken word. Marriages thrive or disintegrate with the spoken word. So short-story writers use dialogue to make characters live for the readers.

In addition to revealing character, dialogue also helps to develop plot. Characters may express opinions or tell about events, and in so doing, they further the conflict.

EXAMINING THE CHARACTERISTICS

Writing successful dialogue demands special attention to the techniques. In general, dialogue

—shows the speaker's exact words by enclosing them in quotation marks,

—includes spelling clues to indicate dialect or speech patterns,

—produces natural-sounding conversation, using short sentences and contractions, as appropriate to the character,

—may include sentence fragments to illustrate a speaker's exact words or to enhance style,

—uses phrases like "he yelled" or "she snarled" to allow readers to "hear" the words in the context of the situation,

—relies heavily on accurate punctuation, including commas, end marks, and apostrophes, as well as quotation marks,

—shows a change in speaker by a change in paragraphing,

—includes description, not just of voice and expression but also of mannerisms and other nonverbal means of communication.

The remainder of this chapter tells you how to produce successful dialogue.

LISTENING TO THE CHARACTER

If you are writing about a real person, you have a responsibility to quote accurately. Since the short story character is fictional, however, you must listen in your mind. Ask yourself the questions below, and then make sure the speech pattern is consistent with the character. For instance, a well-educated character is not apt to use poor grammar, but an uneducated character may not use poor grammar either. He or she may have learned by listening. If, then, you show evidence of his or her having learned other things by listening, it may be out of character to use poor grammar. Let your character talk with others and listen with your mind's ear. Perhaps you can mimic the talk, record it, and then write it from the recording. Make notes as you listen for the answers to the following questions:

—What is the person's usual vocabulary? Does word choice suggest education or lack of it? Are certain words or phrases often repeated, such as "well, actually," "generally speaking," or "well, I declare"?

—Are the sentences short and choppy or moderately long? Does the person answer "Yep" instead of "Yes, I think so"?

—What tone of voice does the speaker usually use? Does he or she shout, whisper, rasp, hiss, or whine?

—Does the character occasionally use poor grammar?

—Does the person drop word endings, saying "walkin' " for "walking" or "talk" for "talked"?

—Does pronunciation reflect a dialect, with words like "cain't" or "musta" for "can't" or "must have"?

WATCHING THE CHARACTER

Dialogue tags often describe mannerisms and other nonverbal means of communication. As a result, when you listen, either in real life or in your mind's ear, you must also watch. Make notes as you ask yourself questions like these:

—How does the character stand or sit? Does he or she slouch, lean on a cane, prop chin in hands? How else can you describe posture?

—What does the character do with his or her hands? Does he jab the air with a pipe-filled fist; does she unceasingly rub her thumbs together, worry with her wedding band?

—How can you describe the person's eyes? Are they clear or cloudy, sparkling or dull? Do they pierce the listener or wander off into an undefined distance?

—What visual evidence is there of facial reaction to comments? A frown, a fading dimple, a grin, a cocked head, a dropped jaw?

—What visual evidence is there of other physical reactions to comments? A shifting of position, crossing a leg, folding the arms, leaning forward?

RECORDING THE CONVERSATION

Regardless of the context in which the dialogue appears, the writing process is the same:

—Write the exact words of the speaker, including spellings that will help readers hear the pronunciation of the words.

—Use sentence fragments as appropriate or necessary to enhance characterization or maintain style.

—Enclose the speaker's words in quotation marks.

—Add descriptions that will help readers hear the tone of voice or vocal inflections.

—Add descriptions that will help readers see the speaker's nonverbal reactions.

—Start a new paragraph each time a new character speaks.

CHECKING THE CONTENT

Read the dialogue aloud, perhaps with a friend or friends who will read other characters' parts. Listen carefully to the dialogue, asking yourself these questions:

—Does the conversation sound natural? Have I avoided a stilted, awkward, uncharacteristic speech pattern?

—Does the conversation fit the character? Are his words and sentences appropriate for his age, sex, education, environment, occupation, and emotional attitude?

—Will readers be bored with too much irrelevant conversation, or is every part essential to furthering the plot or the characterization?

—Is the dialogue snappy, to the point, avoiding lengthy speeches or lengthy sentences?

Make whatever changes you can to improve the natural conversation flow and still achieve your purpose.

CHECKING THE TECHNIQUES

Certain techniques peculiar to writing dialogue require attention beyond the usual checks for grammar, mechanics, and usage:

—Check paragraphing. You may include description relating to the character or the situation in the same paragraph with his or her quoted words, but you must begin a new paragraph when another character begins speaking.

EXAMPLE:

"Have you read the current issues of these magazines?" Jennifer asked, holding up three magazines I'd never seen before.

"No. Why do you ask?" I responded. I really wondered if she would think less of me for not having read the latest issues or for not being at all familiar with the publications.

"Well, that's a good test of your character!"

"What do you mean?"

She stood grinning at me, understanding that she was teasing me and waiting for me to catch on. "You're in the wrong generation to appreciate these magazines!"

I wonder if she thinks I'm too young or too old.

HINT:

In the example above, we know who spoke the words even if the speaker's name does not appear. Because the paragraph changes with each speaker, we can follow the alternating pattern. Effective dialogue makes use of the paragraphing to omit frequent parenthetical identification and thus makes the dialogue move more quickly.

—Check quotation marks. Have you enclosed the speaker's words, but not his thoughts, in quotation marks?

Example:

"So what do you want me to do first?" he asked.

Krista thought he sounded almost willing to help. She hesitated, looked at him again, frowning, unsure why he seemed so helpful. "Why don't you sort the reports by department code?" she suggested. Silently she added, "We'll see if you have any idea what you're doing."

HINT:

Note the difference between thoughts and interior monologue. Thoughts are *not* enclosed in quotation marks; interior monologue is.

Thought:	Krista thought he sounded almost willing to help.
Interior Monologue:	Silently she added, "We'll see if you have any idea what you're doing."

—Check quotation marks around speaker's words that run more than one paragraph. Have you opened each new paragraph with quotation marks but closed the quotation marks only when the speaker finishes?

EXAMPLE:

Karlton was on my case. I tried to maintain my composure as his tirade continued.

"Whatever happens, it goes on record that I have warned you about your behavior. It's been less than admirable. According to my file, your supervisor has talked with you repeatedly about your apparent lack of concentration, your tardiness, your long lunch hours. You know that we simply cannot continue to tolerate such behavior in this office. In fact, I doubt that any other office supervisor would be as patient as we have been.

"But if you have a problem, we'll try to help. Maybe you have something to say that will explain your behavior. If you have some temporary crisis, some unusual stress, some personal problem, let's talk about it."

Karlton finally stopped talking and looked at me. Well, it was more like he looked straight through me. What was I to say? That I'd held up the bank and no one even suspected me? That's hardly a temporary crisis. Maybe unusual stress, but definitely not temporary. I sat stock still, listening to the clock tick.

—Are commas, question marks, and exclamation marks used in correct relationship with the quotation marks?

General Rules:

1. Commas and periods go inside quotation marks.
2. Colons and semicolons go outside quotation marks.

EXAMPLE:

The travel host explained, "You will ride in air-conditioned coaches through the city"; but she neglected to admit that the air conditioning would not be turned on.

3. Question marks and exclamation marks go inside the quotation marks if the quotation itself is a question or exclamation. Otherwise, question marks and exclamation marks go outside the quotation marks.

EXAMPLE 1:

Paula asked, "Are Yuppies really rich?"

EXAMPLE 2:

Did Paula say, "Yuppies are really rich"?

4. Use only one mark of punctuation (besides the quotation mark itself) at the end of a quotation.

EXAMPLES:

Incorrect: "The ceremony included three speakers, and boy, were they boring!," Willard complained.
(Do not use both a comma and an end mark at the close of a quotation.)

Corrected: "The ceremony included three speakers, and boy, were they boring!" Willard complained.

Corrected: "The ceremony included three speakers, and boy, were they boring," Willard complained.

—Are apostrophes used to show omission of letters or dropped endings?

EXAMPLES:

"Are you goin' to the annual reunion?" Martin asked.
"I reckon I'm goin' if the crick don't rise," came the playful response.

—Are spellings appropriate for the dialogue, words in some cases spelled to indicate pronunciation?

—Do capital letters begin not only your sentences but also the sentences of the speakers?

EXAMPLE 1:

Sara explained, "We planned this event well in advance."
(The word *we* is capitalized because the speaker's sentence begins with the quotation.)

EXAMPLE 2:

"This baggage," Tom complained, "must be stuffed with lead!"
(The word *must* is not capitalized because it does not begin the speaker's sentence.)

EXAMPLE 3:

The manager began, "The work in the department has attracted the attention of upper-level management. They hope," he continued, "you will show the other departments how it's done."
(The word *the* is capitalized because it begins the speaker's sentence. On the other hand, *you* is not capitalized because it merely continues the sentence which began with the word *they*.)

REMEMBER:

The speaker's words are set off not only with quotation marks, but also with commas. Note the use of commas in the previous examples.

—Are any grammar or usage errors within the dialogue intentional, designed to characterize the speaker?

—Are narrative and descriptive sections free from grammar and usage errors?

If you use the process above and proofread carefully, you should be able to develop satisfactory dialogue.

STUDYING SAMPLE DIALOGUE

The following sample dialogue is appropriate for fiction.

WATCHING

Clarence leaned into the oars, looking at but not seeing the pink polish on Irene's bare toes. The wind tore at the boat's direction, aiming it to the east of the inlet.

"Don't you think we'll be gettin' there afore long?" An edge of fear slipped into her words, belying her masked smile.

"Aye, we'll be there soon." A long silence bore down between them, lengthened by the distant rumble, the screech of oarlocks, and the seemingly interminable rhythm of dip-splash, dip-splash, dip-splash. "Yep, we'll be there soon."

She studied his face, his averted eyes, and wondered if he was lying. The western sky roiled. He watched her pink-painted toes grip her sandals. No use looking up. He knew too well the creases between her eyebrows and the worry lines on her forehead, even the weak smile that usually accompanied her worry lines.

"We have some water left," she said, "in the thermos here. Don't you want a drink? You're working so hard." He knew she was trying to be helpful and supportive, in spite of her fears. But he couldn't dare stop rowing, the wind as it was.

"Not just yet. But have some yourself," he added.

She loosened the top, tipped up the thermos, took two swallows and wiped the dribble from her chin. She wasn't thirsty, and the water had no taste. "It's still cold. Sure you don't want some?" He shook his head; she closed the thermos.

The sky, like some smothering blanket, hung above them, threatening.

She looked over her shoulder, allowing the bluster to wrap her hair across her face. "We're almost there!"
He heard the relief in her voice. "Yep, we'll make it now." She heard the "now" and knew.

ANALYZING THE SAMPLE

The dialogue above, while it relates only a minor incident, includes examples that illustrate these aspects of dialogue:

—The actual words in the conversation are minimal.

—The dropped endings and word choices help readers "hear" the conversation, the voices, the inflections, and the dialect.

—Sentence fragments, while infrequent, aid in developing a natural-sounding conversation.

—The facial expressions, the nonverbal mannerisms, and the characters' thoughts tell more than the words. Readers can infer all kinds of details: the couple know each other well; he knows what her face looks like without looking; he sees her toes give away her fears; each recognizes the underlying unspoken messages behind the other's actual words; she suspects when he's lying; she recognizes "now" as an affirmation of his effort to comfort her earlier.

—The paragraphing allows readers to follow the speakers without "he said" or "she said" after every quotation mark.

—Description and narration, developed in the paragraph structures, help readers follow the meanings behind the words—the fears, the suggestions, the mindless comments.

—Good description, that which shows rather than tells, helps readers see, hear, feel, and taste the details.

—Accurate punctuation and capitalization help readers follow the dialogue.

Using the process, model, and analysis above, develop dialogue that follows these suggestions. You should have a satisfactory product.

CHAPTER EIGHT

Using Description

Good description relies on the five senses. Readers should see, hear, taste, smell, and feel. At the same time, good description is synonymous with clarity. It conveys information accurately.

IDENTIFYING GOOD DESCRIPTION

Good description includes the following characteristics:

—an emphasis, either direct or indirect, on the five senses,

—use of figures of speech, especially to enrich the description and to spark reader interest,

—details that support the story's tone and mood,

—vocabulary that clarifies and suits the subject, attitude, and audience,

—colorful language, including specific nouns and vigorous, active verbs,

—omission of superfluous modifiers which lead to flowery language,

—varied sentence structure, which adds appropriate emphasis and enhances the general attitude.

EMPHASIZING THE SENSES

In order to create good description, a writer must, above all, arouse the readers' five senses. Compare the following two passages:

EXAMPLE 1:

Bicycling through the farms of central Illinois left Ken feeling tired and thirsty. He was ready for something cold to quench his thirst.

EXAMPLE 2:

Bicycling for the past nine hours left Ken's eyes blurred to the rows and rows of head-high stalks. The sweet pollen of tasseled corn hung heavy in the afternoon humidity, and only an occasional breeze rustled the rich green leaves. But Ken didn't notice. His upper thigh muscles burned; his calves ached. Still he peddled. "Ah, for a crisp, bubbly cola," he thought. Sweet. Cold. Tingling going down.

Notice that the first example *tells*: Ken is bicycling "through the farms of central Illinois," and he feels "tired and thirsty," "ready for something to quench his thirst."

The second example, however, uses sensory images to *show* how Ken feels: exhausted. How do readers know? They know that Ken has been bicycling "for nine hours," and that in spite of the beautiful rows of crops with the sweet aroma of tasseling corn, Ken hardly notices his surroundings. (The location is implied.) Readers also know Ken's exhaustion from sensory images like "his upper thigh muscles burned, his calves ached," and they know Ken's thirst because of his thoughts about a "crisp, bubbly cola."

Which senses are aroused?

Sight: blurred, rows of head-high stalks, rich green
Smell: sweet aroma of tasseled corn
Touch: breeze, heavy humidity, burning muscles, aching calves, cold,
          bubbly, tingling going down
Sound: rustled
Taste: crisp, sweet, cold

HINT:

Use of the five senses will help you show, rather than tell, readers about your characters and their conflicts.

USING FIGURES OF SPEECH

Some writers rely heavily on figures of speech. The most common figures of speech include the following:

metaphor a figure of speech that suggests likeness by speaking of one thing as if it were another. **Example:** Her moods are *the endless myriads of a kaleidoscope.*

simile a figure of speech in which one thing is compared to another, using the word *like* or *as*. **Example:** His muscles were *as loose as last year's slingshot.*

personification a figure of speech in which a thing or idea is represented as a person. **Example:** The sunshine *brushed my face with a warm hand.*

hyperbole exaggeration used for effect, not meant literally. **Example:** He's been teaching in that school *for a hundred years.*

symbol a thing that stands for another thing; especially an object that stands for an idea, quality, etc. **Example:** Is the senator a *dove* or a *hawk?*

alliteration repetition of a beginning sound, usually of a consonant, in two or more words of a phrase, line of poetry, etc. **Example:** *full fathom five* thy *father* lies.

assonance likeness of sound, especially of vowels, as in a series of words or syllables. **Example:** l*a*te and m*a*ke

onomatopoeia the formation of a word by imitating the sound associated with the object or action. **Example:** *chickadee* and *clang*

SUPPORTING TONE AND MOOD

Tone results from the narrator's attitude. From the story's tone, readers can make inferences about characters and plot. Mood is the prevailing spirit or feeling in a piece of writing. In general, tone comes from the narrator's point of view, and that, in turn, helps create mood, which is the effect the piece creates in the readers' minds.

Compare tone and mood in the following two passages:

EXAMPLE 1:

Crashing down the stairs, Marietta hit the door like a lightning bolt and tore blindly across the nearly vacant street. The rain and her tears coursed down her face.

EXAMPLE 2:

Solitude. A loon, unseen in the distance, laughed, and she felt the muscles start to relax in the back of her neck. She wiggled her bare toes in the icy water, unmindful of childhood warnings that she'd catch cold. Her mother's voice echoed in her mind.

The two passages illustrate very different tones and moods. In the first, the harsh verbs *crashing*, *hit*, and *tore* help establish a tone of frustration, perhaps anger. The mood is violent, disturbing, anxious. In the second, the tone of relaxation is furthered by the call of the loon and the character's breaking away from parental guidance. The mood is one of expectancy, wondering what will happen as a result of the breaking away.

POSSIBLE PITFALL:

Be sure to establish a consistent tone and mood throughout the story. Let the tone help reflect character, setting, and plot. The result will be a clearly established mood for readers.

CHOOSING SUITABLE VOCABULARY

Word choice creates tone. For instance, to say that a character is childish is very different from saying he or she is child-like. A word's connotation—the emotional overtone in a word's meaning—directly affects tone. Check a thesaurus to help you choose the most precise word. Compare the following examples:

EXAMPLE 1:

Crashing down the stairs, Marietta hit the door with exploding force and tore blindly across the nearly vacant street. The rain and her tears coursed down her face.

EXAMPLE 2:

Dashing down the stairs, Marietta pushed open the door and ran across the quiet street. The rain and her tears flowed down her face.

The vocabulary in Example 1 is forceful, noisy, explosive. In Example 2, however, the vocabulary softens. Likewise, the tone softens. Marietta is more quiet, so the mood is less disturbing, less violent, more sorrowful.

Consider this second pair of examples:

EXAMPLE 1:

Solitude. A loon, unseen in the distance, laughed, and she felt the muscles start to relax in the back of her neck. She wiggled her bare toes in the icy water, unmindful of childhood warnings that she'd catch cold. Her mother's voice echoed in her mind.

EXAMPLE 2:

Alone. A loon, unseen in the distance, called to its mate, and she felt the loneliness swell. Mindlessly, she let her bare feet hang over the dock's edge and into the icy water, childhood warnings about catching cold long gone from her thoughts.

The vocabulary again changes the tone and mood of the passage. In Example 1 the mood is playful, fun, laughing, carefree, relaxing. In Example 2 the mood is lonely, sad, brooding, detached. So the mood changes from happy to sad, from positive to negative, only because of word choice.

USING COLORFUL LANGUAGE

When a writer selects the details to support tone and mood, he or she also takes a big step toward using colorful language. But other techniques will also credit an author as a skillful wordsmith:

—A good writer uses specific nouns rather than general nouns with one or more modifiers.

EXAMPLE:

| General, weak nouns: | A young child picked up his soft, cuddly toy. |
| Specific nouns: | A toddler picked up his teddy bear. |

—A good writer uses vigorous verbs rather than general verbs with one or more modifiers.

EXAMPLE:

| General, weak verb: | He walked slowly across the yard. |
| Vigorous verb: | He ambled across the yard. |

—A good writer uses active voice verbs rather than passive voice.

EXAMPLE:

| Weak, passive voice: | The whole pie was eaten by our guest. |
| Strong, active voice: | Our guest ate the whole pie. |

HINT 1:

Notice that in the course of using strong, colorful language, a writer will necessarily omit superfluous, flowery modifiers.

HINT 2:

The best description is clean, simple, and direct. It shows rather than tells.

CREATING GOOD SENTENCE STRUCTURE

Whole books have been written about creating good sentence structure. The following list provides only quick guidelines:

—Use a variety of sentence types: simple, compound, complex, and compound-complex. (See the Glossary for definitions and examples.) Varied sentences let you create emphasis.

—Begin your sentences in a variety of ways. For instance, begin some with the subject while you begin others with an introductory phrase or introductory clause. Without variety, your writing will sound dull and monotonous.

—Use a variety of modification structures: words (adjectives and adverbs), phrases (prepositional, participial, infinitive), and clauses (adjective and adverb). (See the Glossary for definitions and examples.)

—Vary the lengths of your sentences. For instance, a short sentence after several long ones gives punch to an idea. Because many writers tend to write sentences of similar length, varying the length usually requires a conscious effort. A mere word count gives a quick check.

—Be sure your main ideas are in main clauses. Put supporting ideas in subordinate clauses.

—Create emphasis by putting important ideas at the ends of sentences. Let sentences build suspense.

—Use good transitions to help readers follow your characters and plot.

—If you use items in a series, use parallel structure. (See the Glossary.)

—Avoid dangling and ambiguous modifiers. (See the Glossary.)

EXAMINING A SAMPLE

The following sample description illustrates most of the characteristics of good descriptive writing. Study the sample and then read the analysis which follows.

THE CEDAR CHEST

As she propped open the hinged lid carved with the traditional hearts and doves, the sweet aromatic cedar scent wafted up, filling the room like incense with a home-at-last comfort. Inside the cedar chest lodged the material realities of the bride's dream for a happy home. In the far left corner, a Trail to Dublin quilt lay folded, its tiny stitching attesting to the work of family quilting bees, its red and white now dimmed in the candlelight. Crowded against it, as if for protection, a pair of pewter candlesticks, still free from wax, stood like sentinels, ready to grace the bride's table. An Aladdin oil lamp, its chimney wrapped in tissue, squatted against the quilt but closer to the front, away from the pewter. The lamp's shining nickel bowl distorted the reflection of the embroidered table runner, folded carefully on top of the knotted comforter to the right. In the far right corner, the precious family heirlooms awaited, linen-wrapped, the new bride's home: a hand-carved springerle board, the family Bible, an ivory comb and brush set, and a floral picture made of hair. She lowered the lid to the chest with a soft bump as wood closed against wood, and she traced with her finger the date carved on the front: 1892.

ANALYZING THE SAMPLE

The description above includes good imagery and figurative language. Note these specifics:

—Images affect most of the five senses. The absence of the other sense, taste, seems reasonable in light of the topic. Note these images:

- Sight: carved, traditional hearts and doves, Trail to Dublin quilt, tiny stitching, red and white dimmed, candlelight, pewter, free from wax, Aladdin oil lamp, wrapped in tissue, stood against the quilt, closer to the front, shining nickel, distorted reflection, embroidered, knotted comforter, linen-wrapped, hand-carved springerle board, Bible, ivory comb and brush set, floral picture made of hair, date on front read 1892

- Smell: aromatic cedar scent, incense
- Touch: propped, carved, crowded against it, tissue, shining lamp bowl, knotted comforter, traced date
- Sound: soft bump of wood against wood

—Figures of speech help readers see more than the specific details:

- Simile: like sentinels, like incense
- Personification: attesting to, crowded, squatted, lay, awaiting
- Alliteration: sweet cedar scent, happy home, pair of pewter, reflection of runner, lay linen-wrapped

—Details are sufficient to clarify the subject and support the nostalgic tone of the piece.

—Active voice and action verbs add emphasis: propped, wafted, stood, squatted, distorted, lowered, traced

—Organization follows a spatial order, from left to right.

—Transitions help readers follow the order, from the opening of the lid, from left to right inside the chest, and then to the outside front.

—Sentence structure varies from simple to complex.

—Since a single attitude prevails, it helps maintain unity throughout the paragraph.

CHAPTER NINE
Beginning and Ending
the Story

A writer's most demanding task is creating an effective story beginning. Busy readers don't finish stories they cannot "get into" quickly. Editors won't read a story that does not grab their immediate attention.

WRITING THE BEGINNING

Because a short story is so brief, the beginning, or exposition, must accomplish four goals within the first few paragraphs:

—It must immediately catch the reader's attention.

—It must draw the reader into your character's world.

—It must establish the tone.

—It must begin the conflict.

As you begin your own short story, then, consider three possible ways to grab your readers:

1. Use dialogue that begins to reveal character and setting and that leads to an initial conflict.

EXAMPLE:

"They're not landing on me."

"That's 'cause you used too much bug spray," whispered Brian.

"But I washed it off," replied Andrew, who started to raise his arm to his nose for a double-check.

"Shhh!" hissed Todd, his older brother.

The tent crossbar, and the flashlight suspended from it, rocked gently in the night breeze, swinging the dirty cone of light first toward Andrew, then around in a loop to catch the tight faces of Brian and Todd, and then again to Andrew's, before re-settling in the middle, bright upon their bare, extended arms.

SLAP!

"What'd you do that for!" Todd demanded without lifting his eyes.

The opening dialogue gives readers clues about the setting, characters, and conflict. Almost as soon as readers know that the two main characters are brothers, they know that the boys are engaged in sibling rivalry. In addition, a few details in the fifth sentence reveal setting.

2. Involve the main character in action that leads to initial conflict.

EXAMPLE:

> Emile bent close over the page, leaning his weight on the crayon to force out a thick blue line. Slowly, his fingers slid down the waxy length until their tips brushed against the page. He relaxed his grip, allowing his mottled hand to regain its color, and scrutinized his scattered pile of crayons and colored pencils. . . .
> He looked up at the clock. Almost two. He was going to be late. After creeping down the broken stairs, he ducked into the kitchen, sneaked a potato from the burlap bag beneath the sink, and slipped out the side door into the alley.

Readers meet the main character alone in the midst of drawing. Immediately, then, the writer establishes the character's creativity. The action that follows, Emile creeping in to sneak a potato, establishes that there is some kind of conflict, and it will lead directly to the initial conflict with his peers. (See the remainder of the story in Chapter Ten.)

3. Establish the setting, giving sufficient details to create the atmosphere.

EXAMPLE:

> The thin motel walls kept out the howling cold but not the all-night grumbling of diesel engines on the interstate. A hot shower would have helped warm her numbed fingers and toes. It was just that the room, with soiled carpets, sagging drapes, burned-out lamp bulb, and worn bedspread, made her feel too vulnerable to take off her clothes.

Here, the setting takes on significance. The main character is revealed in an atmosphere of cold loneliness, emphasized by the shabbiness of the room. Whatever happens will be directly related to these miseries.

WRITING THE ENDING

The short story's ending should do the following:

—fulfill your plot plan.

—show whatever change your main character undergoes as a result of his or her conflict.

—satisfy the reader.

Writers use a variety of methods to end a short story. The following are probably the most common:

1. Simply resolve the conflict so that the reader feels satisfied with the ways things turn out.

Edgar Allan Poe, the master story teller, often simply resolves the conflict. In "The Cask of Amontillado," one character seeks revenge by walling up his enemy in an underground vault. The final lines of the story follow:

> I hastened to make an end of my labor. I forced the last stone into its position; I plastered it up. Against the new masonry I re-erected the old rampart of bones. For the half of a century no mortal has disturbed them. *In pace requiescat!*

2. Allow the reader a glimpse, a recognition that helps him understand the theme of your story.

James Thurber's "The Secret Life of Walter Mitty" uses an ending that reinforces the story's theme. Walter Mitty lives his real life with a domineering wife, but he lives his "secret life," his imaginary life, as a hero. Read the final few sentences from the story:

> Walter Mitty lighted a cigarette. It began to rain, rain with sleet in it. He stood against the wall of the drugstore, smoking. . . . He put his shoulders back and his heels together. "To hell with the handkerchief," said Walter Mitty scornfully. He took one last drag on his cigarette and snapped it away. Then, with that faint, fleeting smile playing about his lips, he faced the firing squad; erect and motionless, proud and disdainful, Walter Mitty the Undefeated, inscrutable to the last.

3. Provide a surprise ending, maybe even an ironic twist that brings the story to a close.

Guy de Maupassant was a master at writing surprise endings. In his story "The Necklace," a woman works most of her life to pay for replacing a jeweled necklace she borrowed and lost. Years later, haggard from hard work, she meets again the woman from whom she borrowed the jewels:

> "You say you bought a diamond necklace to replace that other one?"
> "Yes. You didn't even notice then? They really were exactly alike."
> And she smiled, full of a proud, simple joy.
> Madame Forestier, profoundly moved, took Mathilde's hands in her own.
> "Oh, my poor, poor Mathilde! Mine was false. It was worth five hundred francs at the most!"

Consider the ending of the model short story "Mosquito":

> On a level track, a professional sprinter can run a hundred yards in under ten seconds. Across the plowed field, Andrew wouldn't have been far behind. He crashed through the tent flap, his lungs heaving, his cup down to a half-inch of worm-infested mud, and his animal smile slashing at the faces of the older boys, whose card game his violent entry had upset.
> He grimaced at Todd.
> "Truth or Dare?!" He could already picture Todd gagging as he tried to force down the slimy mud to uphold his forthcoming end of the bargain.
> Again, that sly smile brushed Todd's face as he read through his brother's excitement.
> "Truth," he replied.

The ending completes the plot line. It also generates a double surprise. Andrew completes the Dare and returns to the tent, having met the challenge to measure up, to fit in with the older boys. But the older brother alters his usual "Dare" answer to "Truth," thus dashing the younger's plan to retaliate. Readers see a young boy growing up, having changed sufficiently to meet this immediate challenge but still never quite winning. But even in the ending, the writer is careful to maintain consistent characterization. Todd's sly smile, seen earlier in the story, helps readers remember Todd's primary traits. In spite of Andrew's success in the Dare, his immature behavior when he crashed through the tent flap gives away his plan to his perceptive brother.

POSSIBLE PITFALL:

Be sure to maintain consistent characterization in the ending. Your reader will be suspicious of a contrived change in character to meet some surprise resolution to the conflict.

For an additional example of another story ending, see the model "Spud" in Chapter Ten.

Examining a Model Short Story

The following sample short story serves as a representative model by which we can discuss specifically, in the analysis, many of the generalities we have listed earlier.

SPUD

by David Ciepley

Emile bent close over the page, leaning his weight on the crayon to force out a thick blue line. Slowly, his fingers slid down the waxy length until their tips brushed against the page. He relaxed his grip, allowing his mottled hand to regain its color, and scrutinized his scattered pile of crayons and colored pencils.

Yellow is for sickness
Blue is for sadness
Green is for envy
Black is for badness.

He looked up at the clock. Almost two. He was going to be late. After creeping down the broken stairs, he ducked into the kitchen, sneaked a potato from the burlap bag beneath the sink, and slipped out the side door into the alley. He ran between the crumbling buildings to an abandoned lot where the neighbor boys, lined up with their backs to the wind, were building a fire. They yelled at him across the field to hurry and to pick up some broken lumber for the fire along the way.

"Got your spud?" asked Melby.

"Yeah!"

"Throw 'er in."

They all tried their best to sneak away on Saturday afternoons with a potato or two. Then they sat around the hissing flames for an hour, discussing the cusses Mrs. Yakov had yelled down at her husband from their apartment window, or where Felix had been while he hookied, or who they thought Mrs. Brubaker was going to flunk in spelling, until the potatoes were thoroughly baked beneath the embers.

"Dibs on ya!" Emile yelled, as Melby accidentally uncovered his potato with his poking stick.

"No more dibs!" Melby yelled back, lest anyone else lay claim to a portion of his spud.

Each boy prepared to remove his potato as slyly as possible, scraping around in the coals to find it. Emile had this game all worked out. Instead of scraping the embers, he gently poked them, lowering the risk of accidentally exposing his spud as Melby had. Feeling the tip strike the spud's charred shell, he sidled it underneath and violently flipped the potato out of the fire with an accompanying rain of cinder and smoke that made his companion's eyes water.

"No dibs, no hunks!" he shouted while the potato was still in midair. Then he sat down to his meal.

In school, Mrs. Brubaker wrote long lists of words on the board while the class stared at the clock and yawned. Emile doodled in his spelling book. When Mrs. Brubaker turned around, the rest of the class straightened up, pretending to be awake, but Emile kept on doodling.

"Emile Gallois!"

He jerked upright. "Yes, Ma'am!" and fixed his gaze on the reflections in her spectacles. All at once, her face shifted and buckled, falling into a mosaic of angles and distortion. He averted his eyes.

"Look at me when I'm talking to you!"

Thankfully, the image had disappeared. "Yes, Ma'am."

"Spell 'attentive.' "

"A-t-t-e-n-t-i-v-e."

"Very good. Now *be* attentive."

She turned back to the board and Emile turned back to his doodles. He drew her face as it had seemed, slipping her nose across the side of her cheek, skewing her eyes one way, her wire-rimmed spectacles the other, rolling her scalp forward and her right ear around until all sides of her head appeared superimposed on the flat surface of the page. He drew back to examine the drawing and slapped the book shut.

That weekend, he sneaked a potato as usual, but he didn't go to the field. He tiptoed back up to his room and flipped to the doodled page of his spelling book. With his rusty pocket knife, he began carving Mrs. Brubaker's head. He remembered the reflections in her eye-glasses and released them from their frames, letting the classroom ceiling beams crash into her brow, the ceiling panels slide onto her forehead, and the heavy tendrils of the window-box philodendrons creep through her hair, until her whole face was filled with foreign objects. Then he drizzled water color not too carefully onto her various parts—red on her brow, blue on her forehead, green on her lips—but left the majority of her surface to the yellow pallor of drying potato flesh. In the corner of his bottom drawer he nestled it—the first.

In homeroom Monday morning, Melby approached.

"Where were you?"

"Huh?"

"Saturday?"

Ever since moving into the neighborhood, Emile found himself designated as Melby's playground rival, and he quickly fell under Melby's exacting surveillance.

"I didn't feel well."

"What?"

"I was sick."

"So. What'd you do, draw all day? You should have come."

"My mom wouldn't let me."

"Well, are you gonna play ball after school, or what?"

"Yeah, I'll be there."

"Good. Four o'clock."

At lunchtime, Emile picked at the peanut butter sandwich his mother had packed for him, and he ended up throwing it all in the trash. His stomach bothered him throughout the rest of the afternoon, and he found himself even too distracted to chase the dusky images—of a rugby ball, or Melby's ruddy face, or Mrs. Brubaker's carved head—flitting before his eyes.

On the way to his last class, Emile stepped into the bathroom to heave up yellow stomach bile. He then proceeded straight to his classroom desk where he laid his head. Did he want to go home? No. Or lie down in the cloak room? No. He didn't stir until the bell rang the close of school. Then he lifted himself up and began the walk home.

On the edge of a run-down park, a rotten limb had fallen, and Emile stopped to examine its shattered length. He pulled free a short, fat segment near the base and chipped at its surface with his thumbnail. It was soft, but not yet rotting. Just then, Melby accosted him from the other side of the street.

"You're coming, right?"

"Yeah." He tucked the chunk of wood beneath his arm and continued on, parallel to Melby, but never glancing over or saying a word. At the end of the street, they turned in opposite directions, each proceeding down his own alley.

Emile walked through the empty house up to his bedroom and stuck the chunk of wood in his drawer. After changing into a dirty sweater, he returned downstairs, nibbled at a piece of biscuit, and started for the lot. Several others were already there, including Melby.

"Hurry up, Emile!" he shouted. "You and me are gonna be captains!"

After a half dozen more neighborhood kids had straggled in, the boys chose up sides and started the game.

It was a friendly game—tackle of course, but not too hard, especially since the lot was strewn with gravel and scrap wood. Emile, however, felt Melby was getting a little overzealous.

"Cool it," he told him.

The next play, Emile was passed the ball, and darting a glance to his left, he saw Melby, a curl in the corner of his lip, bearing down on him. Emile dished off the ball, but Melby didn't stop, smothering Emile in his sweater as they rolled onto the ground. The curl of Melby's lip broadened into a jeer. Emile didn't say a word. Instead, on the next play, he went straight for Melby, put his fist into his chest, grabbed his arm, and flung him to the ground. Melby skidded across the gravel on his stomach and then lay still, moaning. Everybody stopped where they stood and gaped. Emile smiled and pretended that he had done it in sport, but when he saw Melby's nose bleeding, he backed up a few steps, turned, and ran home.

He mounted the steps to his room and, curling into a ball, buried his head beneath his pillow. The images returned—the rugby ball, Melby, Mrs. Brubaker. He remembered the chunk of wood he had in his drawer, and pulling out his pocket knife, his hands went to work on it. He knew what he was carving, but he didn't let himself think about it, concentrating instead on the minuteness of the wood grain. The features began to pronounce themselves—a high, square forehead, a pair of dimpled cheeks, a broad flaring chin—and slowly, the hard lines melted into a point between the eyes . . . where his blade came to a knot. He sawed at it with the blade's edge, bored at it with the tip, but the knot was like steel. In desperation, he gouged his blade beneath its edge in an effort to pry it out, but its roots ran deep, and the whole left side of the face splintered away. Underneath, invisible fungi were slowly eating their way outward, rendering the wood useless. A single saline drop splashed onto the rotten vein of wood as he walked to the window. Leaning over the window ledge, he let the half-carved head drop from his hands onto the cobblestones below. One by one, the stars awoke to a quiet street, where a young boy stared down at the scattered pieces of a chunk of wood.

ANALYZING THE MODEL SHORT STORY

The short story above includes all the essentials of the literary form. Note specifically these details:

—The title suggests the significance of the potato not only to the circle of boys who roasted them but particularly to Emile who applied his artistic talents to them.

—The writer never tells his readers where the story takes place. The multi-ethnic names (Yakov, Gallois, and Brubaker) suggest a large city. References to the alley, the crumbling buildings and an abandoned lot also suggest city, perhaps a neighborhood not too prosperous. The boys' first names (Melby and Felix) suggest 1930's or 1940's.

—The only developed character is Emile. Melby, who serves as the antagonist, simply represents boys in general, boys who cannot understand Emile's interest in art.

—Readers are not told about characters; readers see characters in action, hear them, watch them interact.

—The result is consistent, believable characters.

—The dialogue reflects realistic conversation, so it includes grammar-usage errors and sentence fragments. The brevity, candor, and idioms appropriate for children add to realistic character development.

—The writer uses the third-person point of view *narrative* consistently to tell the story from Emile's point of view, no doubt the most appropriate for the message. We know Emile's thoughts and are inside his mind.

—Two conflicts emerge in the story, one within Emile and one between Emile and Melby. The inner conflict is undoubtedly the larger one. Emile, whose artistic insight differentiates him from his schoolmates, must choose either to remain "one of the guys" or to develop his talent. Developing his talent causes ridicule from his peers, but remaining one of the guys results in internal frustration, even illness. His attempt to integrate the two by carving a realistic sculpture of Melby fails—his is a talent requiring external and internal abstraction.

—Emile realizes the failure, and the story concludes with Emile, now much more self-aware, facing the choice as to which of the two ways of life he wishes to lead.

—The Picasso-like faces that emerge in his spelling book and on the potato, representing the art world, contrast with the realistic carving he tries but cannot complete in the wood.

—The story plot can be outlined as follows:

Emile realizes he is different—draws Mrs. Brubaker in his spelling book.
Emile experiments with the artistic life—shirks his friends to carve the potato.

Emile tries to go back to his old way of life—plays football. The effort brings frustration.

Emile tries to integrate the two lives—carves the realistic wooden head. The effort fails.

Emile realizes the failure—drops the carving out the window.

Emile contemplates the choice—stares down at the scattered wood.

—The crisis occurs when Emile bloodies Melby's nose. The physical battle parallels the conflict Emile encounters within himself.

—When the carving splinters (as a result of the fungi, which signifies, too, the rotting friendship between Emile and Melby), the climax leads quickly to the resolution, Emile's realization (as signified by his tears and his dropping the remains of the carving to the street below) that he must choose between his friends and the life of an artist.

—By the end of the story, the potato becomes symbolic. It carries Emile from childhood through the pain of self-discovery, from the roasting fire to the carving hidden away, from physical to spiritual value—from food to art. The potato now symbolizes Emile's growth.

—A message develops from Emile's actions: Those who deal with creative processes—from computer programmers to philosophers—must often choose between their buddies and their art; the choice is never painless.

—Thus, the imagery and figurative language are assets to the story.

—Uncomplicated sentence structure shows good variety and adds emphasis.

—Punctuation is accurate.

—Paragraphing is appropriate for dialogue.

—Description is concise, the result of an effective narrative style. Specific details show, rather than tell, about Emile's daily life.

—Tone and mood remain consistent throughout.

—The conclusion leaves readers without a decision, but the world goes on; the stars come out. The readers are whisked from Emile's room to the street and, logically, to the larger world where people face similar problems, perhaps without any more satisfactory solutions, only the recognition that life demands choices.

Certainly you will make other observations about the story that will arouse your interest or curiosity or that will give you ideas for developing your own short story.

Applying the list of general characteristics, the explanation of process, and the ideas you have gleaned from the sample and its analysis, you should be able to create a reasonably successful imaginative piece of writing.

CHAPTER ELEVEN

Checking Your Story

When you have completed a draft of your short story, you are ready to analyze your work. The analysis will help you polish the rough edges and otherwise hone your story into a fine piece of writing.

REVISING YOUR STORY

You can ask questions, the answers to which will help you spot certain weaknesses. Try these questions on your story:

ABOUT THE BEGINNING

—Does the beginning immediately catch my readers' attention?

—Does the beginning draw readers into my characters' world?

—Does the beginning establish the tone?

—Does the beginning start the conflict?

ABOUT THE CHARACTERS

—Are my characters believable?

—Do their actions fit their personalities?

—Does their dialogue fit their personalities?

—Are they clearly motivated?

ABOUT THE SETTING

—Is the setting suitable for the characters?

—Is the setting suitable for the conflict?

—Does the setting contribute to the mood or atmosphere?

ABOUT THE POINT OF VIEW

—Did I select the most appropriate point of view by which to convey my message?

—Have I maintained consistent point of view?

ABOUT THE PLOT

—Does the conflict result from likely causes?

—Are time relationships clear?

—If I use a flashback, do the transitions assure readers' understanding of the time sequence?

ABOUT THE DIALOGUE

—Is the dialogue natural?

—Is the dialogue consistent with characterization?

ABOUT THE DESCRIPTION

—Have I avoided telling my readers about characters, motives, reactions? Instead, do I show?

—Have I included good sensory details?

—Have I used effective figures of speech?

—Do my descriptive details support the tone and mood?

—Does the vocabulary suit the subject, attitude, and audience?

—Have I used colorful language, including specific nouns and vigorous, active verbs?

—Have I omitted superfluous, flowery modifiers?

—Does my sentence structure add emphasis and variety?

ABOUT THE ENDING

—Does the resolution grow naturally out of the conflict?

—Is the ending satisfying to the readers?

—Have I resolved the characters' conflicts?

ABOUT THE THEME

—Is my message clear to my readers when they finish the story?

—Have I avoided telling the message, allowing it instead to reveal itself through the action and resolution of the story?

—Will readers care about my characters and their conflict?

—Have I selected an appropriate title that suggests some important element of the story?

Revise your story as many times as necessary to make it smooth, readable, and believable.

PROOFREADING THE FINAL DRAFT

No matter how "creative" you think a short story may be, do not be creative with the standards of the language. While characters may speak a nonstandard dialect to convey their backgrounds, your writing must reflect accuracy if you hope it to be accepted. Check the following:

DIALOGUE

—Have I enclosed speakers' words in quotation marks?

—Have I changed paragraphs with each change of speaker?

—Are other marks of punctuation used in correct relationship with quotation marks?

—Did I capitalize correctly?

CHECK OTHER PUNCTUATION

SPELLING

—If words in dialogue appear in nonstandard spellings, do the spellings aid in characterization?

GRAMMAR AND USAGE

—Did I remember to make the descriptive narrative grammatically correct even if dialogue includes certain nonstandard elements to reflect character?

Using this process should help you get at least a running start in the development of your own short story.

Part 3

Beyond the Basics

CHAPTER TWELVE
Analyzing a Master

You have studied the basic components of the short story: theme, plot, setting, characters. You have also studied some of the finer writing techniques for developing short stories: choosing the most effective point of view, developing strong description, and creating dialogue that both reveals character and develops plot. Finally, you have examined two student models.

Now, let's turn our attention to a literary master of the short story. By analyzing a literary model, you should be able to improve your basic story-writing techniques. You need to ask yourself, "What elements in this short story give it the enduring qualities of fine literature? What makes it a classic?" When you answer these questions and apply the answers to your own writing, in essence you begin to imitate the literary masters. Then, as your skills improve, your own writing style will emerge. Short story writing will become an art.

The story which follows was written in the early nineteenth century by Nathaniel Hawthorne (1804–1864), a New Englander who came from a long line of Salem, Massachusetts, residents. One ancestor, in fact, was a presiding judge at the 1692 Salem witch trials, and the guilt Hawthorne associated with that relationship influenced his writing. To distance himself from the family reputation, Hawthorne added the *w* to his name. Nevertheless, his Puritan principles are evident in the following story, especially as the main character searches for perfection.

Even though he was heavily influenced by this Puritan background, Hawthorne was also attracted to the Transcendentalist philosophy. Hawthorne's stories, however, reflect a darker, less cheerful view than that of a true Transcendentalist, but the Transcendentalist's investigation into thought processes is evident in the following story.

Hawthorne, like Edgar Allan Poe, believed the short story must have a "single effect"; but unlike Poe, Hawthorne believed a short story must have a romantic element. The following selection, set in the late 1700s, illustrates Hawthorne's characteristic style—the single effect with a romantic element.

With these brief background notes in mind, study the following story. Watch for the writing techniques that seem to make the story work. When you finish reading, we will do a careful analysis of the author's approach.

THE BIRTHMARK

by Nathaniel Hawthorne

(1)   In the latter part of the last century there lived a man of science, an eminent proficient in every branch of natural philosophy, who not long before our story opens had made experience of a spiritual affinity more attractive than any chemical one. He had left his laboratory to the care of an assistant, cleared his fine countenance from the furnace smoke, washed the stain of acids from his fingers, and persuaded a beautiful woman to become his wife. In those days when the comparatively recent discovery of electricity and other kindred mysteries of Nature seemed to open paths into the region of miracle, it was not unusual for the love of science to rival the love of woman in its depth and absorbing energy. The higher intellect, the imagination, the spirit, and even the heart might all find their congenial ailment in pursuits which, as some of their ardent votaries believed, would ascend from one step of powerful intelligence to another, until the philosopher should lay his hand on the secret of creative force and perhaps make new worlds for himself. We know not whether Aylmer possessed this degree of faith in man's ultimate control over Nature. He had devoted himself, however, too unreservedly to scientific studies ever to be weaned from them by any second passion. His love for his young wife might prove the stronger of the two; but it could only be by intertwining itself with his love of science, and uniting the strength of the latter to his own.

(2)   Such a union accordingly took place, and was attended with truly remarkable consequences and a deeply impressive moral. One day, very soon after their marriage, Aylmer sat gazing at his wife with a trouble in his countenance that grew stronger until he spoke.

(3)   "Georgiana," said he, "has it never occurred to you that the mark upon your cheek might be removed?"

(4)   "No, indeed," said she, smiling; but perceiving the seriousness of his manner, she blushed deeply. "To tell you the truth it has been so often called a charm that I was simple enough to imagine it might be so."

(5)   "Ah, upon another face perhaps it might," replied her husband; "but never on yours. No, dearest Georgiana, you came so nearly perfect from the hand of Nature that this slightest possible defect, which we hesitate whether to term a defect or a beauty, shocks me, as being the visible mark of earthly imperfection."

(6) "Shocks you, my husband!" cried Georgiana, deeply hurt; at first reddening with momentary anger, but then bursting into tears. "Then why did you take me from my mother's side? You cannot love what shocks you!"

(7) To explain this conversation it must be mentioned that in the center of Georgiana's left cheek there was a singular mark, deeply interwoven, as it were, with the texture and substance of her face. In the usual state of her complexion—a healthy though delicate bloom—the mark wore a tint of deeper crimson, which imperfectly defined its shape amid the surrounding rosiness. When she blushed it gradually became more indistinct, and finally vanished amid the triumphant rush of blood that bathed the whole cheek with its brilliant glow. But if any shifting motion caused her to turn pale there was the mark again, a crimson stain upon the snow, in what Aylmer sometimes deemed an almost fearful distinctness. Its shape bore not a little similarity to the human hand, though of the smallest pygmy size. Georgiana's lovers were wont to say that some fairy at her birth hour had laid her tiny hand upon the infant's cheek, and left this impress there in token of the magic endowments that were to give her such sway over all hearts. Many a desperate swain would have risked life for the privilege of pressing his lips to the mysterious hand. It must not be concealed, however, that the impression wrought by this fairy sign manual varied exceedingly, according to the difference of temperament in the beholders. Some fastidious persons—but they were exclusively of her own sex—affirmed that the bloody hand, as they chose to call it, quite destroyed the effect of Georgiana's beauty, and rendered her countenance even hideous. But it would be as reasonable to say that one of those small blue stains which sometimes occur in the purest statuary marble would convert the Eve of Powers to a monster. Masculine observers, if the birthmark did not heighten their admiration, contented themselves with wishing it away, that the world might possess one living specimen of ideal loveliness without the semblance of a flaw. After his marriage,—for he thought little or nothing of the matter before,—Aylmer discovered that this was the case with himself.

(8) Had she been less beautiful,—if Envy's self could have found aught else to sneer at,—he might have felt his affection heightened by the prettiness of this mimic hand, now vaguely portrayed, now lost, now stealing forth again and glimmering to and fro with every pulse of emotion that throbbed within her heart; but seeing her otherwise so perfect, he found this one defect grow more and more intolerable with every moment of their united lives. It was the fatal flaw of humanity which Nature, in one shape or another, stamps ineffaceably on all her productions, either to imply that they are temporary and finite, or that their perfection must be wrought by toil and pain. The crimson hand expressed the ineludible grip in which mortality clutches the highest and

purest of earthly mould, degrading them into kindred with the lowest, and even with the very brutes, like whom their visible frames return to dust. In this manner, selecting it as the symbol of his wife's liability to sin, sorrow, decay, and death, Aylmer's sombre imagination was not long in rendering the birthmark a frightful object, causing him more trouble and horror than ever Georgiana's beauty, whether of soul or sense, had given him delight.

(9)   At all the seasons which should have been their happiest, he invariably and without intending it, nay, in spite of a purpose to the contrary, reverted to this one disastrous topic. Trifling as it first appeared, it so connected itself with innumerable trains of thought and models of feeling that it became the central point of all. With the morning twilight Aylmer opened his eyes upon his wife's face and recognized the symbol of imperfection; and when they sat together at the evening hearth his eyes wandered stealthily to her cheek, and beheld, flickering with the blaze of the wood fire, the spectral hand that wrote mortality where he would fain have worshipped. Georgiana soon learned to shudder at his gaze. It needed but a glance with the peculiar expression that his face often wore to change the roses of her cheek into a deathlike paleness, amid which the crimson hand was brought strongly out, like a bas-relief of ruby on the whitest marble.

(10)   Late one night when the lights were growing dim, so as hardly to betray the stain on the poor wife's cheek, she herself, for the first time, voluntarily took up the subject.

(11)   "Do you remember, my dear Aylmer," said she, with a feeble attempt at a smile, "have you any recollection of a dream last night about this odious hand?"

(12)   "None! none whatever!" replied Aylmer, starting; but then he added, in a dry, cold tone, affected for the sake of concealing the real depth of his emotion, "I might well dream of it; for before I fell asleep it had taken a pretty firm hold of my fancy."

(13)   "And did you dream of it?" continued Georgiana, hastily; for she dreaded lest a gush of tears should interrupt what she had to say. "A terrible dream! I should wonder that you can forget it. Is it possible to forget this one expression?—'It is in her heart now; we must have it out!' Reflect, my husband; for by all means I would have you recall that dream."

(14)   The mind is in a sad state when Sleep, the all-involving, cannot confine her spectres within the dim region of her sway, but suffers them to break forth, affrighting this actual life with secrets that perchance belong to a deeper one. Aylmer now remembered his dream. He had fancied himself with his servant Aminadab, attempting an operation for the removal of the birthmark; the the deeper went the knife, the deeper sank the hand, until at length its tiny grasp appeared to have caught hold of

Georgiana's heart; whence, however, her husband was inexorably resolved to cut or wrench it away.

(15) When the dream had shaped itself perfectly in his memory, Aylmer sat
in his wife's presence with a guilty feeling. Truth often finds its way to
the mind close muffled in robes of sleep, and then speaks with uncompromising directness of matters in regard to which we practise an un-
conscious self-deception during our waking moments. Until now he had
not been aware of the tyrannizing influence acquired by one idea of his
mind, and of the lengths which he might find in his heart to go for the
sake of giving himself peace.

(16) "Aylmer," resumed Georgiana, solemnly, "I know not what may be
the cost to both of us to rid me of this fatal birthmark. Perhaps its
removal may cause cureless deformity; or it may be the stain goes as
deep as life itself. Again: do we know that there is a possibility, on any
terms, of unclasping the firm grip of this little hand which was laid upon
me before I came into the world?"

(17) "Dearest Georgiana, I have spent much thought upon the subject,"
hastily interrupted Aylmer. "I am convinced of the perfect practicability
of its removal."

(18) "If there be the remotest possibility of it," continued Georgiana, "let
the attempt be made at whatever risk. Danger is nothing to me; for life,
while this hateful mark makes me the object of your horror and disgust—
life is a burden which I would fling down with joy. Either remove this
dreadful hand, or take my wretched life! You have deep science. All the
world bears witness of it. You have achieved great wonders. Cannot you
remove this little, little mark, which I cover with the tips of two small
fingers? Is this beyond your power, for the sake of your own peace, and
to save your poor wife from madness?"

(19) "Noblest, dearest, tenderest wife," cried Aylmer, rapturously, "doubt
not my power. I have already given this matter the deepest thought—
thought which might almost have enlightened me to create a being less
perfect than yourself. Georgiana, you have led me deeper than ever into
the heart of science. I feel myself fully competent to render this dear
cheek as faultless as its fell; and then, most beloved, what will be my
triumph when I shall have corrected what Nature left imperfect in her
fairest work! Even Pygmalion, when his sculptured woman assumed life,
felt no greater ecstasy than mine will be."

(20) "It is resolved then," said Georgiana, faintly smiling. "And, Aylmer,
spare me not, though you should find the birthmark take refuge in my
heart at last."

(21) Her husband tenderly kissed her cheek—her right cheek—not that
which bore the impress of the crimson hand.

(22) The next day Aylmer apprised his wife of a plan that he had formed
whereby he might have opportunity for the intense thought and constant

watchfulness which the proposed operation would require; while Georgiana, likewise, would enjoy the perfect repose essential to its success. They were to seclude themselves in the extensive apartments occupied by Aylmer as a laboratory, and where, during his toilsome youth, he had made discoveries in the elemental powers of Nature that had roused the admiration of all the learned societies in Europe. Seated calmly in this laboratory, the pale philosopher had investigated the secrets of the highest cloud region and of the profoundest minds; he had satisfied himself of the causes that kindled and kept alive the fires of the volcano, and had explained the mystery of fountains, and how it is that they gush forth, some so bright and pure, and others with such rich medicinal virtues, from the dark bosom of the earth. Here, too, at an earlier period, he had studied the wonders of the human frame, and attempted to fathom the very process by which Nature assimilates all her precious influences from earth and air, and from the spiritual world, to create and foster man, her masterpiece. The latter pursuit, however, Aylmer had long laid aside to unwilling recognition of the truth—that our great creative Mother, while she amuses us with apparently working in the broadest sunshine, is yet severely careful to keep her own secrets, and, in spite of her pretended openness, shows us nothing but results. She permits us, indeed, to mar, but seldom to mend, and, like a jealous patentee, on no account to make. Now, however, Aylmer resumed these half-forgotten investigations; not, of course, with such hopes or wishes as first suggested them; but because they involved much psychological truth and lay in the path of his proposed scheme for the treatment of Georgiana.

(23)   As he led her over the threshold of the laboratory, Georgiana was cold and tremulous. Aylmer looked cheerfully into her face, with intent to reassure her, but was so startled with the intense glow of the birthmark upon the whiteness of her cheek that he could not restrain a strong convulsive shudder. His wife fainted.

(24)   "Aminadab! Aminadab!" shouted Aylmer, stamping violently on the floor.

(25)   Forthwith there issued from an inner apartment a man of low stature, but bulky frame, with shaggy hair hanging about his visage, which was grimed with the vapors of the furnace. This personage had been Aylmer's underworker during his whole scientific career, and was admirably fitted for that office by his great mechanical readiness, and the skill with which, while incapable of comprehending a single principle, he executed all the details of his master's experiments. With his vast strength, his shaggy hair, his smoky aspect, and the indescribable earthiness that incrusted him, he seemed to represent man's physical nature; while Aylmer's slender figure, and pale, intellectual face, were no less apt a type of the spiritual element.

(26) "Throw open the door of the boudoir, Aminadab," said Aylmer, "burn a pastil."

(27) "Yes, master," answered Aminadab, looking intently at the lifeless form of Georgiana; and then he muttered to himself, "If she were my wife, I'd never part with that birthmark."

(28) When Georgiana recovered consciousness she found herself breathing an atmosphere of penetrating fragrance, the gentle potency of which had recalled her from her deathlike faintness. The scene around her looked like enchantment. Aylmer had converted those smoky, dingy, sombre rooms, where he had spent his brightest years in recondite pursuits, into a series of beautiful apartments not unfit to be the secluded abode of a lovely woman. The walls were hung with gorgeous curtains, which imparted the combination of grandeur and grace that no other species of adornment can achieve; and as they fell from the ceiling to the floor, their rich and ponderous folds, concealing all angles and straight lines, appeared to shut in the scene from infinite space. For aught Georgiana knew, it might be a pavilion among the clouds. And Aylmer, excluding the sunshine, which would have interfered with his chemical processes, had supplied its place with perfumed lamps, emitting flames of various hue, but all uniting in a soft, impurpled radiance. He now knelt by his wife's side, watching her earnestly, but without alarm; for he was confident in his science, and felt that he could draw a magic circle around her within which no evil might intrude.

(29) "Where am I? Ah, I remember," said Georgiana, faintly; and she placed her hand over her cheek to hide the terrible mark from her husband's eyes.

(30) "Fear not, dearest!" exclaimed he. "Do not shrink from me! Believe me, Georgiana, I even rejoice in this single imperfection, since it will be such a rapture to remove it."

(31) "Oh, spare me!" sadly replied his wife. "Pray do not look at it again. I never can forget that convulsive shudder."

(32) In order to soothe Georgiana, and, as it were to release her mind from the burden of actual things, Aylmer now put in practice some of the light and playful secrets which science had taught him among its profounder lore. Airy figures, absolutely bodiless ideas, and forms of unsubstantial beauty came and danced before her, imprinting their momentary footsteps on beams of light. Though she had some indistinct idea of the method of these optical phenomena, still the illusion was almost perfect enough to warrant the belief that her husband possessed sway over the spiritual world. Then again, when she felt a wish to look forth from her seclusion, immediately, as if her thoughts were answered, the procession of external existence flitted across a screen. The scenery and the figures of actual life were perfectly represented, but with that bewitching, yet indescribable difference which always makes a picture, an im-

age, or a shadow so much more attractive than the original. When wearied of this, Aylmer bade her cast her eyes upon a vessel containing a quantity of earth. She did so, with little interest at first; but was soon startled to perceive the germ of a plant shooting upward from the soil. Then came the slender stalk; the leaves gradually unfolded themselves; and amid them was a perfect and lovely flower.

(33) "It is magical!" cried Georgiana. "I dare not touch it."

(34) "Nay, pluck it," answered Aylmer,—"pluck it, and inhale its brief perfume while you may. The flower will wither in a few moments and leave nothing save its brown seed vessels; but thence may be perpetuated a race as ephemeral as itself."

(35) But Georgiana had no sooner touched the flower than the whole plant suffered a blight, its leaves turning coal-black as if by the agency of fire.

(36) To make up for this abortive experiment, he proposed to take her portrait by a scientific process of his own invention. It was to be effected by rays of light striking upon a polished plate of metal. Georgiana assented; but, on looking at the result, was affrighted to find the features of the portrait blurred and indefinable; while the minute figure of a hand appeared where the cheek should have been. Aylmer snatched the metallic plate and threw it into a jar of corrosive acid.

(37) Soon, however, he forgot these mortifying failures. In the intervals of study and chemical experiment he came to her flushed and exhausted, but seemed invigorated by her presence, and spoke in glowing language of the resources of his art. He gave a history of the long dynasty of the alchemists, who spent so many ages in quest of the universal solvent by which the golden principle might be elicited from all things vile and base. Aylmer appeared to believe that, by the plainest scientific logic, it was altogether within the limits of possibility to discover this long-sought medium; "but," he added, "a philosopher who should go deep enough to acquire the power would attain too lofty a wisdom to stoop to the exercise of it." Not less singular were his opinions in regard to the elixir vitae. He more than intimated that it was at his option to concoct a liquid that should prolong life for years, perhaps interminably; but that it would produce a discord in Nature which all the world, and chiefly the quaffer of the immortal nostrum, would find cause to curse.

(38) "Aylmer, are you in earnest?" asked Georgiana, looking at him with amazement and fear. "It is terrible to possess such power, or even to dream of possessing it."

(39) "Oh, do not tremble, my love," said her husband. "I would not wrong either you or myself by working such inharmonious effects upon our lives; but I would have you consider how trifling, in comparison, is the skill requisite to remove this little hand."

(40) At the mention of the birthmark, Georgiana, as usual, shrank as if a redhot iron had touched her cheek.

(41) Again Aylmer applied himself to his labors. She could hear his voice in the distant furnace room giving directions to Aminadab, whose harsh, uncouth, misshapen tones were audible in response, more likely the grunt or growl of a brute than human speech. After long hours of absence, Aylmer reappeared and proposed that she should now examine his cabinet of chemical products and natural treasures of the earth. Among the former he showed her a small vial, in which, he remarked, was contained a gentle yet most powerful fragrance, capable of impregnating all the breezes that blow across a kingdom. They were of inestimable value, the contents of that little vial; and, as he said so, he threw some of the perfume into the air and filled the room with piercing and invigorating delight.

(42) "And what is this?" asked Georgiana, pointing to a small crystal globe containing a gold-colored liquid. "It is so beautiful to the eye that I could imagine it the elixir of life."

(43) "In one sense it is," replied Aylmer; "or, rather, the elixir of immortality. It is the most precious poison that ever was concocted in this world. By its aid I could apportion the lifetime of any mortal at whom you might point your finger. The strength of the dose would determine whether he were to linger out years, or drop dead in the midst of a breath. No king on his guarded throne could keep his life if I, in my private station, should deem that the welfare of millions justified me in depriving him of it."

(44) "Why do you keep such a terrific drug?" inquired Georgiana in horror.

(45) "Do not mistrust me, dearest," said her husband, smiling; "its virtuous potency is yet greater than its harmful one. But see! here is a powerful cosmetic. With a few drops of this in a vase of water, freckles may be washed away as easily as the hands are cleansed. A stronger infusion would take the blood out of the cheek, and leave the rosiest beauty a pale ghost."

(46) "Is it with this lotion that you intend to bathe my cheek?" asked Georgiana, anxiously.

(47) "Oh, no," hastily replied her husband; "this is merely superficial. Your case demands a remedy that shall go deeper."

(48) In his interviews with Georgiana, Aylmer generally made minute inquiries as to her sensations and whether the confinement of the rooms and the temperature of the atmosphere agreed with her. These questions had such a particular drift that Georgiana began to conjecture that she was already subjected to certain physical influences, either breathed in with the fragrant air or taken with her food. She fancied likewise, but it might be altogether fancy, that there was a stirring up of her system—a strange, indefinite sensation creeping through her veins, and tingling, half painfully, half pleasurably, at her heart. Still, whenever she dared to look into the mirror, there she beheld herself pale as a white rose and

with the crimson birthmark stamped upon her cheek. Not even Aylmer now hated it so much as she.

(49)   To dispel the tedium of the hours which her husband found it necessary to devote to the process of combination and analysis, Georgiana turned over the volumes of his scientific library. In many dark old tomes she met with chapters full of romance and poetry. They were the works of the philosophers of the middle ages, such as Albertus Magnus, Cornelius Agrippa, Paracelsus, and the famous friar who created the prophetic Brazen Head. All these antique naturalists stood in advance of their centuries, yet were imbued with some of their credulity, and therefore were believed, and perhaps imagined themselves to have acquired from the investigation of Nature a power above Nature, and from physics a sway over the spiritual world. Hardly less curious and imaginative were the early volumes of the Transactions of the Royal Society, in which the members, knowing little of the limits of natural possibility, were continually recording wonders or proposing methods whereby wonders might be wrought.

(50)   But to Georgiana the most engrossing volume was a large folio from her husband's own hand, in which he had recorded every experiment of his scientific career, its original aim, the methods adopted for its development, and its final success or failure, with the circumstances to which either event was attributable. The book, in truth, was both the history and emblem of his ardent, ambitious, imaginative, yet practical and laborious life. He handled physical details as if there were nothing beyond them; yet spiritualized them all, and redeemed himself from materialism by his strong and eager aspiration towards the infinite. In his grasp the veriest clod of earth assumed a soul. Georgiana, as she read, reverenced Aylmer and loved him more profoundly than ever, but with a less entire dependence on his judgment than heretofore. Much as he had accomplished, she could not but observe that his most splendid successes were almost invariably failures, if compared with the ideal at which he aimed. His brightest diamonds were the merest pebbles, and felt to be so by himself, in comparison with the inestimable gems which lay hidden beyond his reach. The volume, rich with achievements that had won renown for its author, was yet as melancholy a record as ever mortal hand had penned. It was the sad confession and continual exemplification of the shortcomings of the composite man, the spirit burdened with clay and working in matter, and of the despair that assails the higher nature at finding itself so miserably thwarted by the earthly part. Perhaps every man of genius in whatever sphere might recognize the image of his own experience in Aylmer's journal.

(51)   So deeply did these reflections affect Georgiana that she laid her face upon the open volume and burst into tears. In this situation she was found by her husband.

(52) "It is dangerous to read in a sorcerer's books," said he, with a smile, though his countenance was uneasy and displeased. "Georgiana, there are pages in that volume which I can scarcely glance over and keep my senses. Take heed lest it prove as detrimental to you."

(53) "It has made me worship you more than ever," said she.

(54) "Ah, wait for this one success," rejoined he, "then worship me if you will. I shall deem myself hardly unworthy of it. But come, I have sought you for the luxury of your voice. Sing to me, dearest."

(55) So she poured out the liquid music of her voice to quench the thirst of his spirit. He then took his leave with a boyish exuberance of gayety, assuring her that her seclusion would endure but a little longer, and that the result was already certain. Scarcely had he departed when Georgiana felt irresistibly impelled to follow him. She had forgotten to inform Aylmer of a symptom which for two or three hours past had begun to excite her attention. It was a sensation in the fatal birthmark, not painful, but which induced a restlessness throughout her system. Hastening after her husband, she intruded for the first time into the laboratory.

(56) The first thing that struck her eye was the furnace, that hot and feverish worker, with the intense glow of its fire, which by the quantities of soot clustered above it seemed to have been burning for ages. There was a distilling apparatus in full operation. Around the room were retorts, tubes, cylinders, crucibles, and other apparatus of chemical research. An electrical machine stood ready for immediate use. The atmosphere felt oppressively close, and was tainted with gaseous odors which had been tormented forth by the processes of science. The severe and homely simplicity of the apartment, with its naked walls and brick pavement, looked strange, accustomed as Georgiana had become to the fantastic elegance of her boudoir. But what chiefly, indeed almost solely, drew her attention, was the aspect of Aylmer himself.

(57) He was pale as death, anxious and absorbed, and hung over the furnace as it depended upon his utmost watchfulness whether the liquid which it was distilling should be the draught of immortal happiness or misery. How different from the sanguine and joyous mien that he had assumed for Georgiana's encouragement!

(58) "Carefully now, Aminadab; carefully, thou human machine; carefully, thou man of clay!" muttered Aylmer, more to himself than his assistant. "Now, if there be a thought too much or too little, it is all over."

(59) "Ho! ho!" mumbled Aminadab. "Look, master! Look!"

(60) Aylmer raised his eyes hastily, and at first reddened, then grew paler than ever, on beholding Georgiana. He rushed towards her arm with a grip that left the print of his fingers and seized her fingers upon it.

(61) "Why do you come hither? Have you no trust in your husband?" cried he, impetuously. "Would you throw the blight of that fatal birthmark over my labors? It is not well done. Go, prying woman, go!"

(62)   "Nay, Aylmer," said Georgiana with the firmness of which she possessed no stinted endowment, "it is not you that have a right to complain. You mistrust your wife; you have concealed the anxiety with which you watch the development of this experiment. Think not so unworthily of me, my husband. Tell me all the risk we run, and fear not that I shall shrink; for my share in it is far less than your own."

(63)   "No, no, Georgiana!" said Aylmer, impatiently; "it must not be."

(64)   "I submit," replied she calmly. "And, Aylmer, I shall quaff whatever draught you bring me; but it will be on the same principle that would induce me to take a dose of poison if offered by your hand."

(65)   "My noble wife," said Aylmer, deeply moved, "I knew not the height and depth of your nature until now. Nothing shall be concealed. Know, then, that this crimson hand, superficial as it seems, has clutched its grasp into your being with a strength of which I had no previous conception. I have already administered agents powerful enough to do aught except to change your entire physical system. Only one thing remains to be tried. If that fail us we are ruined."

(66)   "Why did you hesitate to tell me this?" asked she.

(67)   "Because, Georgiana," said Aylmer, in a low voice, "there is danger."

(68)   "Danger? There is but one danger—that this horrible stigma shall be left upon my cheek!" cried Georgiana. "Remove it, remove it, whatever be the cost, or we shall both go mad!"

(69)   "Heaven knows your words are too true," said Aylmer, sadly. "And now, dearest, return to your boudoir. In a little while all will be tested."

(70)   He conducted her back and took leave of her with a solemn tenderness which spoke far more than his words how much was now at stake. After his departure Georgiana became rapt in musings. She considered the character of Aylmer, and did it completer justice than at any previous moment. Her heart exulted, while it trembled, at his honorable love—so pure and lofty that it would accept nothing less than perfection nor miserably make itself contented with an earthlier nature than he had dreamed of. She felt how much more precious was such a sentiment than that meaner kind which would have borne with the imperfection for her sake, and have been guilty of treason to holy love by degrading its perfect idea to the level of the actual; and with her whole spirit she prayed that, for a single moment, she might satisfy his highest and deepest conception. Longer than one moment she well knew it could not be; for his spirit was ever on the march, ever ascending, and each instant required something that was beyond the scope of the instant before.

(71)   The sound of her husband's footsteps aroused her. He bore a crystal goblet containing a liquor colorless as water, but bright enough to be the draught of immortality. Aylmer was pale; but it seemed rather the con-

sequence of a highly-wrought state of mind and a tension of spirit than of fear or doubt.

(72) "The concoction of the draught has been perfect," said he, in answer to Georgiana's look. "Unless all my science have deceived me, it cannot fail."

(73) "Save on your account, my dearest Aylmer," observed his wife, "I might wish to put off this birthmark of mortality by relinquishing mortality itself in preference to any other mode. Life is but a sad possession to those who have attained precisely the degree of moral advancement at which I stand. Were I weaker and blinder it might be happiness. Were I stronger, it might be endured hopefully. But, being what I find myself, methinks I am of all mortals the most fit to die."

(74) "You are fit for heaven without tasting death!" replied her husband. "But why do we speak of dying? The draught cannot fail. Behold its effect upon this plant."

(75) On the window seat there stood a geranium diseased with yellow blotches, which had overspread all its leaves. Aylmer poured a small quantity of the liquid upon the soil in which it grew. In a little time, when the roots of the plant had taken up the moisture, the unsightly blotches began to be extinguished in a living verdure.

(76) "There needed no proof," said Georgiana, quietly. "Give me the goblet. I joyfully stake all upon your word."

(77) "Drink, then, thou lofty creature!" exclaimed Aylmer, with fervid admiration. "There is no taint of imperfection on thy spirit. Thy sensible frame, too, shall soon be all perfect."

(78) She quaffed the liquid and returned the goblet to his hand.

(79) "It is grateful," said she with a placid smile. "Methinks it is like water from a heavenly fountain; for it contains I know not what of unobtrusive fragrance and deliciousness. It allays a feverish thirst that had parched me for many days. Now, dearest, let me sleep. My earthly senses are closing over my spirit like the leaves around the heart of a rose at sunset."

(80) She spoke the last words with a gentle reluctance, as if it required almost more energy than she could command to pronounce the faint and lingering syllables. Scarcely had they loitered through her lips ere she was lost in slumber. Aylmer sat by her side, watching her aspect with the emotions proper to a man the whole value of whose existence was involved in the process now to be tested. Mingled with this mood, however, was the philosophic investigation characteristic of the man of science. Not the minutest symptom escaped him. A heightened flush of the cheek, a slight irregularity of breath, a quiver of the eyelid, a hardly perceptible tremor through the frame,—such were the details which, as the moments passed, he wrote down in his folio volume. Intense thought

had set its stamp upon every precious page of that volume, but the thoughts of years were all concentrated upon the last.

(81)   While thus employed, he failed not to gaze often at the fatal hand, and not without a shudder. Yet once, by a strange and unaccountable impulse, he pressed it with his lips. His spirit recoiled, however, in the very act; and Georgiana, out of the midst of her deep sleep, moved uneasily and murmured as if in remonstrance. Again Aylmer resumed his watch. Nor was it without avail. The crimson hand, which at first had been strongly visible upon the marble paleness of Georgiana's cheek, now grew more faintly outlined. She remained not less pale than ever; but the birthmark, with every breath that came and went, lost somewhat of its former distinctness. Its presence had been awful; its departure was more awful still. Watch the stain of the rainbow fading out of the sky, and you will know how that mysterious symbol passed away.

(82)   "By Heaven! it is well-nigh gone!" said Aylmer to himself, in almost irrepressible ectasy. "I can scarcely trace it now. Success! success! And now it is like the faintest rose color. The lightest flush of the blood across her cheek would overcome it. But she is so pale!"

(83)   He drew aside the window curtain and suffered the light of the natural day to fall into the room and rest upon her cheek. At the same time he heard a gross, hoarse chuckle, which he had long known as his servant Aminadab's expression of delight.

(84)   "Ah, clod! ah, earthly mass!" cried Aylmer, laughing in a sort of frenzy, "you have served me well! Matter and spirit—earth and heaven—have both done their part in this! Laugh, thing of the senses! You have earned the right to laugh!"

(85)   These exclamations broke Georgiana's sleep. She slowly unclosed her eyes and gazed into the mirror which her husband had arranged for that purpose. A faint smile flitted over her lips when she recognized how barely perceptible was now that crimson hand which had once blazed forth with such disastrous brilliancy as to scare away all their happiness. But then her eyes sought Aylmer's face with a trouble and anxiety that he could by no means account for.

(86)   "My poor Aylmer!" murmured she.

(87)   "Poor? Nay, richest, happiest, most favored!" exclaimed he. "My peerless bride, it is successful! You are perfect!"

(88)   "My poor Aylmer," she repeated, with a more than human tenderness, "you have aimed loftily; you have done nobly. Do not repent that with so high and pure a feeling, you have rejected the best the earth could offer. Aylmer, dearest Aylmer, I am dying!"

(89)   Alas! it was too true! The fatal hand had grappled with the mystery of life, and was the bond by which an angelic spirit kept itself in union with a mortal frame. As the last crimson tint of the birthmark—that sole token of human imperfection—faded from her cheek, the parting breath of the

now perfect woman passed into the atmosphere, and her soul, lingering a moment near her husband, took its heavenward flight. Then a hoarse, chuckling laugh was heard again! Thus ever does the gross fatality of earth exult in its invariable triumph over the immortal essence which, in this dim sphere of half development, demands the completeness of a higher state. Yet, had Aylmer reached a profounder wisdom, he need not thus have flung away the happiness which would have woven his mortal life of the selfsame texture with the celestial. The momentary circumstance was too strong for him; he failed to look beyond the shadowy scope of time, and, living once for all in eternity, to find the perfect future in the present.

Now that you have read "The Birthmark," let's analyze the story in terms of author technique. We will analyze the story part by part, examining each of the short-story components outlined in this text: theme, characters, plot, setting, point of view, dialogue, and description. The analysis will attempt to define the techniques that give Hawthorne success.

ANALYZING THEME

The theme of "The Birthmark" emerges in the first paragraph:

The higher intellect, the imagination, the spirit, and even the heart might all find their congenial aliment in pursuits which . . . would ascend from one step of powerful intelligence to another, until the philosopher should lay his hand on the secret of creative force and perhaps make new worlds for himself. We know not whether Aylmer possessed this degree of faith in man's ultimate control over Nature.

By the time the story concludes, Hawthorne realizes a key principle: "Thus ever does the gross fatality of earth exult in its invariable triumph over the immortal essence." Aylmer proved that "The momentary circumstance was too strong for him; he failed to look beyond the shadowy scope of time, and, living once for all in eternity, to find the perfect future in the present" (para. 89).

Hawthorne's Puritan heritage is at work. Humans cannot be perfect; only celestial beings can. Thus, to make Georgiana perfect is to make her celestial, i.e., to kill her. Humans in their imperfection cannot create perfection; they cannot imitate the Creator. Furthermore, to try to do so approaches the sinful. As Georgiana says at the end (para. 88), "My poor Aylmer . . . You have rejected the best the earth could offer." Only beyond this earth can anything more perfect exist. She knows that; so does Aylmer, but he discovers it too late.

So is the theme tied to Hawthorne's religious principles? Yes. Is it lofty? Yes. Is it so lofty to be beyond the ordinary reader's reach? No. And therein lies the secret to classic success. Hawthorne, like most other writers, believed that his themes must be relevant to the readers' daily lives. Any of us can follow the story of a husband's wish to make his wife more beautiful. But the theme, of course, goes beyond that. Is it wrong to strive for perfection? Is it deadly? These are universal questions. Hawthorne's theme deals with a man who "in almost irrepressible ecstasy" (para. 82) has been able to remove Nature's blemish. That, according to the story's theme, is wrong: "You came so nearly perfect from the hand of Nature that this slightest possible defect . . . shocks me, as being the visible mark of earthy imperfection" (para. 5). The birthmark becomes the "fatal flaw of humanity" (para. 8) between the husband and his otherwise perfect wife.

Application to Your Own Writing

Does this mean that your own theme must deal with life and death situations or be couched in religious principles in order to have a classic story? No. What it does mean, however, is that the theme must have *universal qualities*. That is, anyone anywhere anytime reading your story must be able to identify with the problem your theme addresses. Certainly life, death, and religion are topics which concern everyone, but other topics are equally pressing. Think of other great pieces of literature you have read and recall their themes: parent-child relationships, husband-wife relationships, sibling relationships, infidelity, bravery, sacrifice, jealousy, envy, unrequited love, disobedience, competition, struggle for success—the list is endless. So, in a nutshell:

> REMEMBER: To have classic qualities, your story's theme must have universal appeal.

ANALYZING CHARACTERIZATION

"The Birthmark" has only three characters: Aylmer, the alchemist; his wife, Georgiana; and Aylmer's servant, Aminadab. The protagonist, Aylmer, is, of course, the most fully developed character. Hawthorne uses a narrator to tell us about Aylmer's character, but we also hear him and see him in action—and his actions do, indeed, speak louder than words.

Aylmer—What He Does

Hawthorne characterizes Aylmer by his passion for science. Everything he does is the result of that obsession; he becomes, in fact, the classic "mad" scientist. For instance, Aylmer's actions show that the scientist's passion, not the husband's, directs his attention to Georgiana's imperfection. His growing, finally overpowering, disgust at his wife's birthmark becomes an obsession. When Georgiana agrees to the removal process, we see a man obsessed by the challenge, regardless of the risks. A man who loves his wife will overlook physical blemishes; a man who loves his wife will not risk her life in an unproven—much less untried—experiment. Aylmer's actions, then, show the love of science overpowering his love of his wife.

Other actions also characterize the obsessed scientist. He records in his folio his experiments—all failures. To reassure Georgiana, he creates two showcase experiments—both failures. He continues to believe, however, that he is capable of the greatest of all successes—to improve upon Nature. This is the "mad" Aylmer, the scientist who will risk the life of another to try one more experiment. Hawthorne includes Aylmer's failures not only to give depth to the character, but also to prepare readers for the story's end.

Aylmer—What He Says

Hawthorne's dialogue lets us hear Aylmer's words supporting the actions of a mad scientist. Let one example suffice to illustrate: "Doubt not my power. . . . You have led me deeper than ever into the heart of science. I feel myself fully competent to render this dear cheek as faultless as its fellow . . . I shall have corrected what Nature left imperfect in her fairest work!" (para. 19). Virtually all of Aylmer's dialogue follows a similar vein. They are the words of a man obsessed.

Aylmer—What Others Say about Him

What else do we know about Aylmer? In the first paragraph, the narrator says that "he had left his laboratory . . . and persuaded a beautiful woman to become his wife" and that "it was not unusual for the love of science to rival the love of woman in its depth and absorbing energy." That exposition lays the groundwork for the readers' interpretation of Aylmer's character. We can expect a struggle between science and marriage.

Aside from the narrator's exposition, the only other insight into

Aylmer comes, of course, from his wife's point of view. Knowing that she is the trusting wife, readers can either rejoice in her love or pity her ignorance; nevertheless, it is through her that we learn the following:

> She considered the character of Aylmer, and did it completer justice than at any previous moment. Her heart exulted . . . at his honorable love—so pure and lofty that it would accept nothing less than perfection. . . . She felt how much more precious was such a sentiment than that meaner kind which would have borne with the imperfection for her sake. . . . (para. 70)

Otherwise, by way of reputation, we know only that Aylmer "had roused the admiration of all the learned societies in Europe" (para. 22). Readers are thus left with the conflict between the veneration of a loving wife and admiring audience and the knowledge of failed experiments of an obsessed, mad scientist.

Aylmer—Comparison Characterization

To help solve the readers' conflict, Hawthorne employs yet another technique of characterization worthy of special note. To help readers think through Aylmer's objection to Georgiana's birthmark, the author compares Aylmer's reactions to those of other men: "Many a desperate swain would have risked life for the privilege of pressing his lips to the mysterious hand" (para. 7). Indeed, "Masculine observers, if the birthmark did not heighten their admiration, contented themselves with wishing it away, that the world might possess one living specimen of ideal loveliness without the semblance of a flaw" (para. 7). By creating these comparisons, Hawthorne further emphasizes Aylmer's scientific passion. Because of it, the aversion to the mark grows "with every moment of their united lives" (para. 8). This character flaw—the pursuit of perfection—leads Aylmer, as well as Georgiana, to destruction.

Georgiana

The other two characters are rather flat. The antagonist, Georgiana exists primarily as the owner of the birthmark. In the course of the story, we have an occasional glimpse of her growing love for, trust in, and worship of Aylmer. Her words and actions unveil her character. The narrator says, "Georgiana, as she read, reverenced Aylmer and loved him more profoundly than ever, but with less entire dependence on his judgment than heretofore" (para. 50). Even though she bursts into tears over Aylmer's failures, she says, "It has made me worship you more than ever" (para. 53). She is later upset that Aylmer has concealed the danger of the procedure (para. 62) and vows, "I shall quaff whatever draught you bring me; but it will be on the same principle that would induce me to take a dose of poison if offered by your hand" (para. 64). We see her as blindly devoted to a man who, although he is her husband, has a poor track record in the work he is about to do. Even when she is about to drink the potion and Aylmer takes time to prove its effects on a plant, Georgiana claims, "There needs no proof. . . . Give me the goblet. I joyfully stake all upon your word" (para. 76). Even Aylmer acknowledges Georgiana's perfection: "There is no taint of imperfection on thy spirit" (para. 77), and she is characterized as Nature's masterpiece (para. 22). We may not see her as a well-rounded woman of the twentieth century, but she isn't intended to be. Her character serves its purpose in the story's theme. Hawthorne's characterization of her is brief, consistent, clear—even if in its flatness it is somewhat stereotypical.

Aminadab

Even more brief, however, is Hawthorne's masterful characterization of the servant Aminadab. We read only a few sentences about the man: "With his vast strength, his shaggy hair, his smoky aspect, and the indescribable earthiness that incrusted him, he seemed to represent man's physical nature. . . ." (para. 25). His voice is "more likely the grunt or growl of a brute than human speech" (para 41), and he obviously lacks any great intellect. We have only a glimpse of him in the laboratory (where he follows directions well but, we're told, never understands the principles) and a final reaction from him in the form of a "gross, hoarse chuckle" which Aylmer knew as Aminadab's "expression of delight." Aylmer himself refers to Aminadab as a "clod," an "earthly mass" (para. 83–84), both expressions indicative of Aylmer's attitude toward Aminadab's station in life. One line, however, lets readers see his humanness: "If she were my wife, I'd never part with that birthmark" (para 27). He may not, in fact, be the ignorant brute Aylmer thinks he is. It is also possible that the line says as much about Aylmer as it does about Aminadab.

Application to Your Own Writing

Hawthorne's characterizations exhibit one trait in common: the most significant aspect of a character's personality is the one most carefully developed. Aylmer is the mad scientist obsessed with perfecting Nature's flaws. Georgiana is the trusting wife. Aminadab is the ignorant servant.

One lesson story writers can learn from Hawthorne's style of characterization is worth emphasizing: Develop a main character whose flaw prepares readers for the story's outcome. Show the character consistently. But, more importantly,

REMEMBER: Don't *tell* your reader about your characters; *show* them.

We aren't *told* that Aylmer is a failure; we see his aborted experiments. We aren't *told* that Georgiana is a trusting wife; we see her unquestioning acceptance of Aylmer's potions. We see the characters through their actions, through their words, and through what others say about them.

ANALYZING PLOT

The parts of plot—exposition, opening incident, rising action, climax, falling action, and resolution—are clearly evident in "The Birthmark." By way of thinking about "plot outline," let's walk through the parts of the plot to see what Hawthorne does to develop this short story.

Exposition

The exposition occurs in paragraphs 1 and 2. In those few lines, readers learn about the setting and the main character's background (scientist recently married) and are forewarned about the usual passion most scientists have for their subjects. In short, the stage is set for the mysteries of alchemy—the recent invention of electricity "and other kindred mysteries of Nature," the furnace smoke and stain of acids, and Aylmer's "higher intellect." The exposition ends in the couple's home "soon after their marriage," with Aylmer about to speak to his wife.

Quickly, then, Hawthorne has involved readers in his plot. Already, perceptive readers find hints of the story's outcome: "He had devoted himself, however, too unreservedly to scientific studies ever to be weaned from them by any second passion" (para. 1).

Opening Incident

The protagonist and antagonist begin the initial conflict almost immediately. Aylmer asks Georgiana if she ever considered that "the mark upon your cheek might be removed" (para. 3). Her reaction—a smile—disappears immediately when she realizes his reaction to the birthmark. While from her point of view the mark "has been so often called a charm" (para. 4), she understands immediately that Aylmer sees it as shocking. That terminology rouses Georgiana's fears: "You cannot love what shocks you" (para. 6).

After this opening incident, Hawthorne steps back to describe the birthmark and others' reactions to it, all of which helps intensify the conflict between husband and wife.

Rising Action

Following the descriptive passages about the mark and Aylmer's growing horror of it, the plot line continues. Georgiana herself brings up the topic late one night to ask about Aylmer's dream the preceding night. At this point, Hawthorne begins what works well for most story tellers: forcing the reader to make inferences. Georgiana's questions about the dream imply that Aylmer must have talked in his sleep, perhaps thrashing about so that Georgiana heard him say, "It is in her heart now; we must have it out" (para. 13). To *tell* readers too much is to insult them; to let them *infer* what has taken place is to entertain them. Hawthorne's plots allow for frequent inferences.

The rising action continues through Aylmer's sharing with his wife a plan for the operation (para. 22) and his finally leading her "over the threshold of the laboratory" (para. 23). Suspense builds as readers follow the plot through the aborted experiments, through Georgiana's insight into Aylmer's failures recorded in his folio, through the first treatment and its failure, through her trip into the laboratory.

The surprise visit to the laboratory creates added conflict. When Aminadab warns the engrossed Aylmer of Georgiana's presence, Aylmer cries, "Would you throw the blight of that fatal birthmark over my labors? It is not well done. Go, prying woman, go!" (para. 61). His agitation is evidenced by his somewhat rough treatment of Georgiana as he hurries her out of the forbidden room "with a grip that left the print of his fingers" (para. 60). Now, remember why Georgiana goes uninvited to the laboratory: to tell Aylmer about a strange sensation in the birthmark. She never tells him; he never knows that his first treatment did, in fact, have some effect. (Perhaps, if given time, it may have removed the blemish; but that is another of Hawthorne's scintillating tidbits from which readers can draw inferences.)

In the course of this disturbing encounter, however, Georgiana assumes a calm that is in deep contrast to Aylmer's agitation: " 'I submit,' she replied calmly," and she proceeds to vow her willingness to drink even poison "if offered by your hand." That statement results in Aylmer's change: " 'My noble wife,' said Aylmer, deeply moved, 'I knew not the height and depth of your nature until now' " (para. 65). That insight sets the stage for the climactic event.

Climax

The climax occurs, of course, when Georgiana actually drinks the liquid. At that point, nothing can reverse the story's outcome. Remember, it is the climax which determines the final outcome. Any time up to Georgiana's drinking the liquid, the ending could have changed. Aylmer could have decided to live with the fault; Georgiana could have refused the drink; Aminadab could have interfered. Once the liquid is down, however, the rest is inevitable.

Notice, then, the care with which Hawthorne builds the suspense. We expect at any moment some turn of events: that something tragic will happen in the laboratory, that Georgiana will experience some insight to change her mind, that knowing the seriousness of the danger, Aylmer may not have the courage to risk his wife's life. Up to the last minute, we look for an out. It never comes.

Falling Action

Some short short stories have no falling action. Here, however, Hawthorne creates a kind of quiet wind-down, almost like a religious experience. Readers know the inevitable outcome. Georgiana sets the scene for her impending death when she says calmly, "Life is but a sad possession to those who have attained precisely the degree of moral advancement at which I stand. . . . I am of all mortals the most fit to die" (para. 73). All that remains is the final quenching of her "feverish thirst" (para. 79), Aylmer's ecstatic reaction to the fading blemish, Aminadab's laugh of delight, Georgiana's murmur of "My poor Aylmer!" (para. 86), and Aylmer's final denial of yet another failure.

Resolution

The resolution comes, of course, with Georgiana's death. Her final line of dialogue says it all: "Aylmer, dearest Aylmer, I am dying" (para. 88). There is no anger, no regret—only perfection ready to rise to the celestial world.

A final paragraph gives Hawthorne an opportunity to express the underlying theme: "The fatal hand had grappled with the mystery of life, and was the bond by which an angelic spirit kept itself in union with a mortal frame." We have to suspect that there is a double meaning in *hand*—the birthmark, and Aylmer's hand in trying to remove it; for he, too, grappled with the mystery of life and Georgiana was his bond between the spiritual and the mortal.

Foreshadowing

As part of the plot, Hawthorne uses dozens of examples of foreshadowing, most of which are evident only after a third or fourth reading—a good clue that the foreshadowing is cleverly done. Consider these examples:

The first paragraph suggests Aylmer's basic philosophy may be his downfall: "He had devoted himself . . . too unreservedly to scientific studies ever to be weaned from them by any second passion." Readers know from the very first where Aylmer's real passions lie.

Also early in the story (para. 8), we read that the birthmark "was the fatal flaw of humanity which Nature, in one shape or another, stamps ineffaceably on all her productions. . . ." The use of the word *fatal* foreshadows the inevitable resolution. In fact, the expression is repeated at the end of the story (para. 89) in the clause "the fatal hand had grappled with the mystery of life."

The next major foreshadowing occurs in the dream discussion (para. 11–15). The dream depicts an operation which finds the hand sinking into Georgiana's body "until at length its tiny grasp appeared to have caught hold of Georgiana's heart; whence, however, her husband was inexorably resolved to cut or wrench it away" (para. 14). We know that the hand does, at least figuratively, clench the heart. The dream becomes reality.

The failed experiments and the folio records, all discussed earlier, also serve as foreshadowing.

The final foreshadowing is, however, probably Hawthorne's most dramatic. Georgiana is musing, rejoicing in Aylmer's "honorable love," when "with her whole spirit she prayed that *for a single moment*, she might satisfy his highest and deepest conception. Longer than one moment *she well knew it could not be* [italics added]. . . ." (para. 70). We know that after the blemish was removed, she lived only *for a single moment*, and in retrospect we are overwhelmed that she drank the liquid *knowing* that it could be no longer than one moment.

The masterful foreshadowing is the mark of a classic story teller.

Application to Your Own Writing

The development of a successful plot is probably the most important aspect of short story writing. Hawthorne's model provides superb examples for your own stories:

—The exposition is brief, establishing setting and the main character's background in a single paragraph. Strive toward that goal in your own stories.

—The opening incident comes quickly, the single conflict of the plot becoming immediately apparent. Successful short stories follow this plan. Aim to follow it, too.

—Rising action continues to build. The suspense grows as a result of the predictions readers can make regarding the outcome; thus, the more intense the rising action, the greater the suspense. Write your own short stories with an eye toward a series of complications that build suspense. Those complications must

• be realistic,

• follow a natural flow of events without too much coincidence, and

• serve to further the plot or show character development.

—The climax, although certainly predictable, leaves readers without hope that something better will happen, that somehow Georgiana will live. The climax in your own story must leave no doubt about the story's outcome. It will result from the one action that determines what *must* happen. Build to it carefully; then resolve the plot quickly.

—The resolution, fulfilling Hawthorne's theme, gives readers a sense of completeness, a knowledge that in her perfection Georgiana died and that Aylmer in his struggle for perfection succeeded— but, at the same time, ironically, failed. The resolution in your own story must fulfill your theme. Readers must be able to go back through your story, look for clues, and be reassured that, based on characterization and the chain of events, this is the inevitable outcome.

—Foreshadowing is so masterful in "The Birthmark" that only on subsequent readings can we recognize that Hawthorne told us all along that the end would be disastrous—unless, of course, you accept the belief that achieving perfection in death is not at all disastrous, but rather, the ultimate good.

Work toward these goals as you develop more artful plots.

ANALYZING SETTING

Hawthorne spends very little time describing the three parts of the story's setting. We know from the exposition that the story takes place in "the latter part of the last century" (para. 1), i.e., the 1700s. We see nothing of the home shared by Aylmer and Georgiana except a reference to its fireplace. We get only a fleeting glimpse of the laboratory with its smoking furnace and maze of "apparatus of chemical research" (para. 56). The setting, then, is mostly atmosphere—a kind of mood established that is consistent with the plot. Much of what readers see in the mind's eye regarding setting must come from inference.

There is one exception to this otherwise cursory attention to details about setting. When Georgiana is moved into the apartment at the laboratory, Hawthorne devotes a rather lengthy paragraph to its description, concluding it "might be a pavilion among the clouds" (para. 28). The description suggests a celestial quality, optical illusions which "appeared to shut in the scene from infinite space." The parallel with heavenly qualities must certainly be intentional, perhaps yet another form of foreshadowing, and certainly in contrast to the laboratory itself.

Hawthorne uses setting, then, to enhance literary qualities we will address later, namely symbolism that offers special treats to careful readers.

Application to Your Own Writing

Follow Hawthorne's model. Unless the setting demands your readers' attention in order to further the plot, build suspense, or create foreshadowing, keep references to a minimum. Readers don't want to read about times and places, they want to read about the conflict, the struggle, the plot, the theme. Give them what they want!

ANALYZING POINT OF VIEW

Hawthorne uses the omniscient third-person point of view, the narrator who knows all and sees all. Thus, we learn about Aylmer's innermost thoughts: "At all the seasons which should have been their happiest, he invariably and without intending it, nay, in spite of a purpose to the contrary, reverted to this one disastrous topic" (para. 9). At the same time, we know how Georgiana feels: "Georgiana began to conjecture that she was already subjected to certain physical influences" (para. 48). We have even some insight into Aminadab as he mutters to himself: "If she were my wife, I'd never part with that birthmark" (para. 27). It is the point of view most suitable to Hawthorne's purpose. If we did not know each character's thoughts, we could misinterpret Hawthorne's theme. We might assume Aylmer has some sinister motive, that Georgiana is a victim of overpowering drugs, that Aminadab adds something to the drink to do away with a woman he seems to admire. Instead, Hawthorne's use of the omniscient third-person point of view eliminates those possibilities.

Application to Your Own Writing

Choosing the point of view most suitable to your purpose is not a matter of coincidence. Plan carefully what clues your readers need, what they must know or need not know. Decide how you can best portray characters—by getting inside their minds or only watching and listening to them, guessing what is going on inside their minds. Which approach will best entertain your readers?

> REMEMBER: Don't tell your readers everything; let them make inferences and enjoy the mental exercise of following your plot, watching your clues, and seeing the inevitable resolution unfold.

ANALYZING DIALOGUE

A very small percentage of "The Birthmark" is made up of dialogue. The dialogue that is included seems stilted because of the old-fashioned language, typical of Hawthorne's literary period. Nevertheless, the dialogue serves two purposes: to further the plot and to develop character. Let's look at just a few examples:

Dialogue to Further the Plot

Hawthorne uses dialogue to further the plot throughout the story. For instance, the opening incident is in dialogue (para. 5), the conversation in which Aylmer admits his aversion to his wife's birthmark. The rising action begins with Georgiana's question to her husband about the dream: "Do you remember, my dear Aylmer, . . . have you any recollection of a dream last night about this odious hand?" (para. 11). It is also through dialogue that Georgiana encourages Aylmer to attempt to remove the mark: "If there is the remotest possibility of it, . . . let the attempt be made at whatever risk. Danger is nothing to me; for life, while this hateful mark makes me the object of your horror and disgust—life is a burden which I would fling down with joy" (para 18). Even in the final moments of the resolution, dialogue reveals the plot: "My poor Aylmer . . . you have aimed loftily; you have done nobly. Do not repent that with so high and pure a feeling, you have rejected the best the earth could offer" (para. 88).

Dialogue to Develop Character

While most dialogue serves to further plot, much of it in the middle of the story also helps readers understand character. For instance, Aylmer assures his wife that "I have already given this matter the deepest thought—thought which might almost have enlightened me to create a being less perfect than yourself" (para. 19). In another case he says, "Believe me, Georgiana, I even rejoice in this single imperfection, since it will be such a rapture to remove it" (para. 30). Through his words, we learn how passionately Aylmer embraces his work. Likewise, Georgiana gives readers a glimpse into her own character: "Spare me not, though you should find the birthmark take refuge in my heart at last" (para. 20). Also, "I joyfully stake all upon your word" (para. 76), and "You mistrust your wife. . . . Think not so unworthily of me, my husband" (para. 62). As a result of her dialogue, we see a strong woman, a wife committed to her husband's passion.

Nonverbal Communication

Hawthorne's descriptions of the characters' actions also help further the plot and develop the characters. For instance, when we read about Georgiana's blushing, her bursting into tears, her fainting, her shrinking "as if a redhot iron had touched her cheek" (para. 40), we draw inferences about emotions and reactions. When we read about Aylmer's cringing, his shuddering, his countenance that was "uneasy and displeased" (para. 52), we draw inferences about underlying motives. By including these instances of nonverbal communication, Hawthorne helps readers "see" characters.

Application to Your Own Writing

Descriptions of nonverbal communication are similar to developing meaningful dialogue. To include meaningful dialogue means you will do what Hawthorne has done: You will make sure there is a purpose for every line of dialogue—either to further plot or to develop character. Chit-chat for the sake of dialogue has no place in a successful short story.

REMEMBER: Use dialogue to further the story—either its plot or the characterization.

ANALYZING DESCRIPTION

Hawthorne's use of description aims toward the "single effect" short story writers have always emphasized. We have already seen evidence that he shows and doesn't tell. We have already seen how his description of nonverbal communication enhances character development. What remains is an analysis of the imagery, figures of speech, tone and mood, and diction in Hawthorne's work.

Imagery

Without a doubt, Hawthorne is sensitive to his readers' reactions to sensory details. All five senses appear in his descriptive details. First, descriptions of Georgiana's blemish evoke visual responses: "In the usual state of her complexion—a healthy though delicate bloom—the mark wore a tint of deeper crimson, which imperfectly defined its shape amid the surrounding rosiness" (para. 7). Second, olfactory responses waft through the descriptions: "She found herself breathing an atmosphere of penetrating fragrance, the gentle potency of which had recalled her from her deathlike faintness" (para. 28). Third, tactile responses are both harsh and gentle: "He rushed towards her arm with a grip that left the print of his fingers and seized her fingers upon it" (para. 60), but "Her husband tenderly kissed her cheek—her right cheek. . . ." (para. 21). Fourth, auditory images rise from Georgiana's "liquid music" that "quench[es] the thirst of [Aylmer's] spirit" (para. 55). Finally, fifth, Georgiana describes her gustatory response to the elixir: "Methinks it is like water from a heavenly fountain; for it contains I know not what of unobtrusive fragrance and deliciousness" (para. 79).

Figures of Speech

Figures of speech add a literary quality to the simplest of stories. Their use should enhance the theme or the mood or tone; they should not appear for the sake of appearance. Hawthorne is particularly astute in his use of similes and metaphors, personification, and symbolism. *Similes* and *metaphors* appear throughout the story. They serve primarily to enhance description, but they also help establish the tone of the work. One metaphor describes Aylmer's obsession with the birthmark: "Trifling as it at first appeared, it so connected itself with innumerable trains of thought and models of feeling that it became the central point of all" (para. 9). Georgiana's explanatory metaphor that "life is a burden" (para. 18) helps us understand the implication of the simile "she beheld herself pale as a white rose" (para. 48) and the continuing comparison: "My earthly senses are closing over my spirit like the leaves around the heart of a rose at sunset" (para. 79). Another metaphor describes Aylmer's professional successes: "His brightest diamonds were the merest pebbles, and felt to be so by himself, in comparison with the inestimable gems which lay hidden beyond his reach" (para. 50). Another metaphor compares Georgiana's singing voice to water: "So she poured out the liquid music of her voice to quench the thirst of his spirit" (para. 55). The frequent use of similes and metaphors adds an intellectual dimension to Hawthorne's work.

Personification likewise gives added dimension to a beautifully structured story. Envy, sleep, truth, and nature are all personified in lines like these:

- "Had she been less beautiful,—if Envy's self could have found aught else to sneer at,—he might have felt his affection heightened. . . ." (para. 8).
- "Sleep, the all-involving, cannot confine her spectres within the dim region of her sway. . . ." (para. 14).
- "Truth often finds its way to the mind close muffled in robes of sleep, and then speaks with uncompromising directness. . . ." (para. 15).
- "I shall have corrected what Nature left imperfect in her fairest work!" (para. 19).

Other examples of personification include the furnace in the laboratory: "The first thing that struck her eye was the furnace, that hot and feverish worker, with the intense glow of its fire. . . ." (para. 56). The most important personification, however, is of the birthmark itself. "Do we know that there is a possibility, on any terms, of unclasping the firm grip of this little hand which was laid upon me before I came into the world?" (para. 16).

Symbolism is part of most fine literature, and "The Birthmark" offers a number of symbols for readers' stimulation. The most obvious symbol, as you might guess, is the birthmark. What Georgiana first thinks of as a "charm" (para. 4) becomes, in the eyes of others, "the bloody hand" (para. 7), symbolic of something evil and life-threatening. Indeed, the "crimson stain upon the snow" (para. 7), another bloody image, appears this time on snow, symbolically pure, as Georgiana. More obviously, Aylmer sees the mark as "the symbol of his wife's liability to sin, sorrow, decay, and death" (para. 8), the "symbol of imperfection" (para. 9). Later, Georgiana refers to the "birthmark of mortality" (para. 73). The resolution concludes the symbolic references: "The fatal hand had grappled with the mystery of life" (para. 89), a double meaning discussed earlier.

Other significant symbols include the characters themselves. Aylmer represents the "spiritual element" (para. 25), a man "reverenced" (para. 50), even "worship[ped]" (para. 53) by Georgiana, who believes that "her husband possessed sway over the spiritual world" (para 32). He is, nevertheless, "burdened with clay . . . thwarted by the earthly part" (para. 50). Aylmer's servant, Aminadab, represents "man's physical nature" (para. 25), the "man of clay" (para. 58). The alchemist and his servant are compared symbolically in Aylmer's exclamation: "Matter and spirit—earth and heaven—have both done their part in this!" (para. 84). On the other hand, Georgiana represents perfection. Her celestial qualities are suggested throughout, but especially in the description that "There is no taint of imperfection on thy spirit" (para. 77). Finally, the "now perfect woman passed into the atmosphere, and her soul, lingering a moment near her husband, took its heavenward flight" (para. 89).

Brief symbolic references also enhance mood. For instance, the apartment is referred to as "a pavilion among the clouds" (para. 28), an obviously heavenly place. It is there in the laboratory, in what Aylmer refers to as "the boudoir" (para. 26) that Georgiana, the bride, reposes and where Aylmer leads her "over the threshold" (para. 23) in groomlike fashion, as if this alchemy act is closer to the consummation of their marriage than any other act.

Tone and Mood

Tone and mood are consistently reflected throughout the story and are directly related in most cases to the setting. The birthmark, referred to as "a frightful object," renders "horror" (para. 8). Aylmer's thoughts "revert" to this topic, and his eyes wander "stealthily to her cheek" where he beholds the "spectral hand that wrote mortality where he would fain have worshipped" (para. 9). Thus, the word choice enhances the mood of repugnance.

The mood changes, however, in the laboratory boudoir. Here, the mood is one of "enchantment," "gorgeous[ness]," "grandeur and grace," "soft, impurpled radiance" (para. 28) where "airy figures, absolutely bodiless ideas, and forms of unsubstantial beauty came and danced before her" (para. 32). It's the alchemist's world of magic.

The mood changes one final time at the climax. Then, all is quiet and calm except for Aylmer's ecstatic exclamations and Aminadab's laughter. Georgiana has a "placid smile" (para. 79), "murmur[s]" (para. 86), and speaks with "more than human tenderness" (para. 88), suggesting her already-angelic qualities. The final mood is one of sadness, the result of knowledge—or at least understanding of knowledge—learned too late. The quiet sadness is marred only by Aminadab's hoarse, chuckling laugh, "the gross fatality of earth [exulting] in its invariable triumph over the immortal essence" (para. 89).

Diction

What makes one author's style most distinctive from another's is a combination of word choice (diction) and sentence structure. While describing an author's style is a rather elusive task, we can make the following general observations about Hawthorne's style as illustrated in "The Birthmark":

Sentence structure tends to be lengthy, involving multiple independent clauses with multiple modifying clauses and phrases. Today, in fact, his language seems lofty if not plain old fashioned. Nevertheless, that is Hawthorne's style.

Word choice, on the other hand, offers a real model for student writers. The connotative meanings (mentioned briefly above) go a long way toward clarifying characters' attitudes as well as establishing the story's changing mood.

Allusion likewise enhances meaning in references like "Even Pygmalion, when his sculptured woman assumed life, felt no greater ecstasy than mine will be" (para. 19) as well as those allusions to "Albertus Magnus, Cornelius Agrippa, Paracelsus, and the famous friar who created the prophetic Brazen Head" (para. 49).

Alliteration softens the final passages and illustrates Hawthorne's fine sense of language: "She spoke the last words with a gentle reluctance, as if it required almost more energy than she could command to pronounce the faint and lingering syllables. Scarcely had they loitered through her lips ere she was lost in slumber. . . . Mingled with this mood, however, was the philosophic investigation characteristic of the man of science. Not the minutest symptom escaped him" (para. 80). The repetition of the soothing consonant sounds of *l*'s and *m*'s soften and quiet the passage.

Application to Your Own Writing

Using good description is essential to the development of a short story, but the description should add more than cumulative details. Hawthorne's description stimulates the readers' intellect with imagery, figurative language, and diction which enhances mood and tone. To do the same is to write effective description.

While imitating another's style is a good way to learn what style is all about, you will eventually concentrate on developing your own. Keep in mind, however, that "style" is not a license for breaking rules; rather, the most important part of style is conscious recognition of good writing. Add to that the use of symbolism, irony, parallel comparisons, inferences, and the other literary techniques we have described, and you will have at least a grasp of style. It's an elusive thing that results only from years of practice and polish. Begin now striving for your own style.

CHAPTER THIRTEEN

Breaking Into Print

Even the most enthusiastic writers lose steam if they have no audience for their short stories. Part of the joy of writing is to entertain readers and revel in their praise. As any entertainer knows, an audience—of one, a dozen, or hundreds—feeds the creative juices, inspires confidence, and sometimes, when comments turn negative, even motivates improvement. A news commentator, a rock band, even the class clown suffocates without an audience. It is the same with a writer. As a result, the final step in the writing process—sharing, or publishing—deserves at least as much attention as the initial steps of preparation and polishing.

Writers, being the creative souls that they are, have discovered ingenious ways of finding—or creating—audiences. Let's examine some of those audiences; you can seek the one best for you.

SEEKING SUPPORT GROUPS

One of the simplest ways to find an audience is to seek out others with similar interests. Sometimes fiction writers band together in small support groups, reading their works to one another, seeking advice, praise, and encouragement. Sometimes they join their fellow non-fiction and poetry writers at conferences to learn, share, support, and celebrate on a larger, more formal scale. Both avenues offer advantages for the novice short-story writer.

Writers' Groups

On a local basis, fellow writers find each other in creative writing classes, in libraries, or through mutual friends. Most who band together in some loosely organized group meet informally, maybe once or twice a month, in living rooms, tea rooms, or coffee houses. Although these informal groups follow no set agenda, they generally engage in one of two routines:

—In some groups, everybody brings something to read from his or her latest endeavors: a plot outline, a single scenario, a series of character sketches, a finished story, or a descriptive paragraph.

—In other groups, some readers share their own writing while others may choose to share an outstanding story they have just discovered in a current magazine, literary journal, or contemporary anthology.

Most readers have a purpose in reading what they have chosen, such as seeking advice about a problem in characterization, plot development, or a technical writing point. They could also be hoping for encouragement or a pat on the back for improvement, or perhaps rejoicing in another author's technical success, characterization, description, or clever plot.

These writers' groups, like any other support group, are only as good as their members. When the group includes avid readers who are familiar with classical as well as contemporary short stories, members profit more than do those in groups whose members simply praise everyone for everything. On the other hand, no group enjoys relentless negativism. As a rule of thumb, then, join or create a group consisting of peers who can recognize and acknowledge the superior elements in a piece of writing, but who can also spot flaws and simultaneously offer alternatives for improvement. In short, look for a group of friendly, supportive editors. Even Stephen King depends on good editors!

Writers' Conferences

While the informality of writers' groups may appeal to many, other writers prefer, at least once or twice a year, to join a more formal contact group. These people frequently turn to writers' conferences—local, state, or regional meetings that last for a weekend, week, or longer. Writers' conferences are often set at a campus or hotel, with concurrent sessions or classes addressing typical writers' interests: writing and marketing fiction, nonfiction, drama, or poetry. While writers' conferences rarely offer classes or concurrent sessions free of charge, from the point of view of most attendees, immersion into the writing atmosphere makes the usually minimal charge worthwhile.

Foremost among the advantages of writers' conferences is the contact with other writers. Inevitably, over early-morning coffee, midafternoon colas, or late-night pizza, writers share war stories. They tell tales about their experiences with editors, their frustrations over long waits for replies, their sources for story ideas, their sense that a story just isn't "working," or their enthusiasm for a peer's characterizations. They share disappointments and celebrate one another's successes. They carry their portable typewriters or lap-top computers and work into the wee hours of the morning, sharing manuscripts and revisions in progress. They seek the muse and take advantage of the inspiration of the moment.

In fact, many conference attendees claim they spend more time in dorm rooms or in coffee shops sharing their manuscripts and ideas with fellow attendees than they do in formal classes or sessions listening to teachers. Nevertheless, it is these classes or sessions that give meat to any writers' conference. Classes are usually taught by respected authors or editors and reflect the talent and experience of these experts. As you might expect, the author- or editor-teacher makes the class, so the primary measure of a successful writers' conference is the quality of author-teachers or editor-teachers it can draw (as conference planners well know).

Be aware, however, that these "teachers" or presenters generally differ from typical classroom teachers—in some good ways and in some not-so-good ways. As experts in their fields of writing and/or publishing, they bring vast knowledge to the conference, knowledge that is yours for the tapping. On the other hand, most have no training in teaching, so their classroom or presentation manner may or may not be conducive to learning. If, however, you attend with the attitude that you have come to learn as much as you can, get your questions answered, and tap the resources, you will make significant strides in spite of—if not because of—the presentation manner. At most writers' conferences small, informal classes provide a comfortable, nonthreatening atmosphere that promotes questions from novices and frank discussion with those more experienced. So students learn not only from the teachers but also from each other.

Beyond the classes themselves are the other "perks" offered to participants during many conferences. Class enrollment at many writers' conferences includes the opportunity to submit manuscripts for personal critiques—an invaluable opportunity unequaled anywhere else. For instance, anyone who is enrolled in the short-story writing class may submit manuscripts in advance, and then during the conference week meet for a critique with the author-/editor-teacher. It's the perfect way to find out what merit another writer (or editor) sees in your work and/or to seek suggestions for improvement and marketing. Innumerable writers got their start—and inspiration—in such settings.

Often, the highlight of a writers' conference features a keynote speaker, usually someone well known as an author, editor, agent, or publisher—and usually someone who can inspire, entertain, and build self-confidence among novice writers. A really good keynote speaker joins conference attendees at an informal reception where participants can chat personally with the keynoter, addressing questions and discussing topics of specific interest to them. To take advantage of such contacts is to gain valuable knowledge. All just for the price of a question!

Of course, not every writers' conference follows the same plan. And certainly some conferences are far better than others. To learn more specifically which conference(s) will best meet your needs, write for information. In writers' magazines like *Writer's Digest*, you will find a list of writers' conferences, their respective dates and locations, and the name and address of a contact person for each. Do some comparison shopping, make your decision, and then take advantage of every second of every minute you have at the conference. You can sleep when you get back home.

FINDING AVENUES FOR PUBLICATION: THE FIRST STEP

Although peer groups and writers' conferences offer meaningful support to struggling authors—novice or otherwise—most writers ultimately decide that such groups are too limited an audience. Just like actors and actresses who want to see their names in lights, writers want to see their names—and their works—in print. They seek publication. No doubt you will want the same! So how do you go about it?

Most writers take the first step at home. High school students submit manuscripts to their high school literary magazine, which is sometimes a class publication or sometimes a school-wide project, published either annually or semi-annually. College students submit manuscripts to their campus newspaper, creative writing or journalism club, or English department literary magazine, which is often a semester or a yearly publication. Other writers submit manuscripts to community and church groups which often publish monthly or quarterly issues of some kind of newsletter or booklet. Having your work appear in these publications does not pay in dollars and cents, but it does count! Being published is a valuable line item on your resume!

FINDING AVENUES FOR PUBLICATION: THE NEXT STEP

Other avenues, beyond the local markets, also offer good opportunities for beginning writers. Keep in mind that for at least three reasons, editors must constantly seek new writers:

—First, no matter how stable their publications, editors must continue to provide fresh ideas from fresh writers if they are to maintain their readership (translation: stay in business).

—Second, editors must replace those former regulars who are no longer productive or have dropped out of the writers' market for whatever reason.

—Third, new magazines hit the market on a regular basis, most designed to meet real or perceived market niches. All need writers.

The trick for a beginning writer, of course, is to hook up with one of these editors looking for new talent.

HOOKING UP WITH AN EDITOR: BECOMING A MAGAZINE DETECTIVE

How does a prospective writer hook up with an editor seeking new talent? The best way is by becoming a magazine detective, analyzing the scene and looking for clues. Several sources help with both the analysis and the clues and are available either from a good library or bookstore. The most common sources include annual publications like *Writer's Market, Writer's Yearbook, Writer's Handbook, Novel and Short Story Writer's Market,* and *Literary Market Place,* as well as monthly magazines like *Writer's Digest* and *The Writer.* All deal with selling and the markets: the annual works are organized by the kinds of magazines described, such as sports, teen, religious, women's, and business, while the monthly magazines focus on changes such as new publications, new editors, and new addresses.

Begin your detective work by studying one of the annual publications like *Writer's Market.* Be sure you're studying a current one, not last year's edition. There are two simple reasons for this bit of advice:

—In the first place, the magazine business changes fairly quickly. Publications merge and are bought and sold; editorial direction and, therefore, advertising images change; editors move; companies change addresses, phone numbers, and so on.

—In the second place, even the current reference was probably in preparation and production for most of a year. That means its information is almost a year old by the time it reaches the bookstore or library shelves.

In short, don't waste time studying old references.

Literary and "Little" Magazines

As you delve into your detective work, one of the first categories to consult in an annual market reference is one usually labeled *literary* or *little* magazines. Writers, especially short-story writers, can gain experience by being published in literary and "little" magazines, which are often published by educational institutions or cultural groups. While these publications generally do not pay for manuscripts (or give as payment free copies of the issue in which the manuscript appears), having a short story in such a publication lends credence to your name as an author. And while these "little" magazines tend to be regional, they are also often quite scholarly, so getting published in one—even without pay—is nothing to sneeze at. In fact, because agents and editors looking for new talent tend to peruse these publications, many literary careers have been launched through the "little" magazines.

To identify the literary and "little" magazines, look in *Novel and Short Story Writer's Market* (published by Writer's Digest Books), where you will find nonpaying fiction markets listed. Or check *Writer's Market* to find listed the more lucrative—but also more competitive—fiction markets.

Regional Publications

As you delve further into your detective work, consider also your own regional publications. Often these publications have fewer writers competing for the limited number of fiction slots available, partly, perhaps, because they tend to pay less than some other consumer magazines. On the other hand, if you are trying to break into print, you may have to accept low pay (or even no pay) to make that first step.

Nevertheless, in spite of their low budgets, regional magazines for the most part maintain highly respected standards. Editors look for material slanted specifically toward the geographic and cultural area. However, many do not accept fiction, so first study the magazine carefully and then request writers' guidelines. The editor for *Now and Then*, for instance, notes that "Everything we publish has something to do with life in Appalachia present and past.... Short stories that convey the reality of life in Appalachia (which can include malls, children who wear shoes and watch MTV) are the kinds of things we're looking for." In other words, know the region well before you consider a submission.

Regional publications have discriminating readers who recognize fallacious details.

Consumer Magazines

If you find no appropriate regional publications, turn to the regular consumer market. The competition is keener here, but if you seek out some of the less well-known publications, your chances are better than if you go for the big names. Continue your detective work by consulting the listings in the consumer sections for the market to which your story seems most likely targeted. For instance, if your characters are teenagers, you will probably seek consumer magazines designed for teen and young adult readers. On the other hand, if your hero is a minority youth, you have another restrictor in your search. Now, instead of general youth magazines, you will probably seek ethnic/minority magazines directed toward young adult readers. Likewise, if your plot revolves around a businessman facing a divorce, seek magazines with readers who can identify with the character and the plot.

HOOKING UP WITH AN EDITOR: ANALYZING THE MAGAZINE SCENE

Once you spot a magazine that seems to have the right readership for your short story, check that it accepts short stories by freelance writers. The most common complaints among editors revolve around the unsolicited manuscripts that arrive on their desks—often manuscripts that are totally inappropriate for the publication—including short stories submitted to publications that have never published short stories. *Read the magazine before you submit any manuscript.*

The entries in *Writer's Market* will clarify a number of policies about each magazine and ultimately save you hours of reading. You may find, for instance, that a magazine uses "two short stories per issue," that it uses "occasional science fiction," that it is "80% freelance written," that it "accepts previously unpublished writers," or that your submission will receive a response "in three months" (a long time when you are checking the mailbox every day). On the other hand, if the magazine's entry does not include a reference to fiction, the editor will not consider any short story, no matter what its quality.

Naturally, the more short stories included per issue, the higher the percentage of freelance work accepted (i.e., work by people not on the publication's staff). And the greater the use of new writers, the better your chances for consideration. Some magazine's entries will give other clues. For instance, *Redbook* editors note that "Of the 40,000 unsolicited manuscripts that we receive annually, we buy about 36 or more stories a year." The odds of 36 to 40,000 are not great, so before you submit a story there, be sure it addresses the target audience: "young mothers between the ages of 25 and 44, most of whom are married with children under 18 and more than half of whom work outside the home."

In addition, be sure to pay attention to all the guidelines and tips offered. For instance, the entry for *Cat Fancy* includes the following notations for fiction: "Adventure, fantasy, historical and humorous. Nothing written with cats speaking." You will waste your time submitting to this magazine a short-story manuscript that does not follow these guidelines. Likewise, the entry for *Hooked on Fishing* offers this tip: "We are looking for fishing stories that keep a family approach to the sport in mind, but with a certain aesthetic appeal beyond hard facts and technical jargon. No good-old-boy fiction." To be accepted, your story *must* follow these guidelines.

HOOKING UP WITH AN EDITOR: LOOKING FOR CLUES IN THE MAGAZINE

When you have found a dozen or so magazines that seem to be likely markets, begin the next part of the detective work: Find copies of the magazines themselves. Two important guidelines should direct your search:

1. Obtain recent issues of every magazine to which you want to submit a short story. Look for the most current on the newsstand, and look for back issues at the library. (Remember that although the library will have the most current issue, you probably cannot check it out. If you cannot or choose not to buy the current issue, you will have to plan time to study the current issue in the library's periodical reading room.) Sometimes, however, if you are seeking less well-known magazines (which, by the way, are the most likely markets for beginning writers), neither the newsstand nor the library may have the issues you need. In that case, try used bookstores. If that, too, fails, send a self-addressed stamped envelope (magazine size) to the publication's address as listed in *Writer's Market* and request several sample issues. Sometimes the *Writer's Market* entry for a given magazine will include

an offer of a free issue upon request, and occasionally even offer a phone number by which to make such a request.

2. Obtain multiple copies of each magazine. How many? If the magazine publishes several short stories in each issue, try to get at least the last four issues. If the magazine uses only one or two short stories in each, try for six issues. Only after studying a series of issues can you make generalizations about the kinds of short stories a magazine will be likely to buy.

When you have copies, begin the more serious detective work of magazine analysis. Take notes as you thumb through the magazine to answer these questions:

—What kinds of goods and services are advertised in the magazine? Sportswear? China and glassware? Travel agencies? Home cleaning aids? Office supplies? Make a list.

—What kinds of people buy and use these products? Men? Women? Athletes? College students? Travelers? Computer users?

—How old are the target members?

Remember that these answers indicate the magazine's target audience, so your story must appeal to this readership.

—What kinds of regular features (sometimes called "departments") appear in the magazine? Profiles? Psychology? Sports? Home remedies? New software analyses? Music, art, or theater reviews? Vacation tips? Education? The singles scene? Gourmet recipes? Guides to great hunting? Fashion trends? Real estate buys?

Remember that this analysis helps pinpoint the editorial slant for the magazine, and your story, to be accepted, must meet the same editorial slant.

—In addition to the regular features, what kinds of articles appear in each issue? How to remodel the garage? Ways to plan a great vacation? Activities that improve church attendance? How to meet the perfect mate? Foods that keep you healthy?

These features are chosen by the editorial staff to reflect the perceived interests of readers, so your observation of these interests should help you determine whether or not your story matches the editorial needs of the magazine.

—What is the general appearance of the magazine? What appears on the covers? What image do the photographs convey? Slick and modern? Conservative? Avant-garde? Art Deco?

Does the appearance further identify the kind of readership the magazine targets?

ANALYZING PUBLISHED SHORT STORIES

When you have uncovered all the general clues, turn to the short stories themselves. Here your research becomes even more detailed. Make a chart of your responses to the following questions to help guide your detective work:

—Do you find different authors represented in every issue? If so, you can assume the editors accept work from a variety of writers rather than relying on a favorite few.

(On the other hand, I know from personal experience that editors sometimes publish stories under pseudonyms to conceal the fact that they use the same few writers over and over. I once had the peculiar experience of having three works published in a single issue, each credited to a different name! So, nothing is certain in this business.)

—Who are the short-story writers? Are they male or female? Is their gender concealed by the use of initials instead of first names?

As you analyze the magazine's authorship, ask yourself certain questions: does it seem unlikely, if you are male, that you can sell a short story to a magazine whose readership is mostly female? Does it seem unlikely, if you are female, that you can sell a short story to an outdoor/adventure magazine? Does it seem necessary to conceal your gender with the use of initials if you hope to sell?

—Who are the characters in the published stories? Are they male or female? Young or old? What are their environments? What problems do they face?

Remember that editors choose short stories that their readers can identify with, and the fictional characters often reflect the readership.

—What are the settings? Are they consistent? Are they the kind of settings that readers can identify with? Or are they the kind that readers can only dream about?

—What types of stories appear? Science fiction? Romance? Adventure? Detective/murder mysteries? Confession?

—What themes are represented? Are they values-related? Work-related? Family-related?

—What writing styles do the stories follow? Do they use simple sentence structure? Colloquial expressions? Scholarly language? Ethnic dialects? Technical jargon?

When you have completed analyzing the stories, draw generalizations about the kinds of stories most likely to be accepted by each publication. You then have several choices:

1. Select the publication whose stories most resemble your own.
2. Revise your story to make it more suitable for a given publication.
3. Begin fresh, writing specifically for a market that appeals to you.

It should go without saying that no editor wants a rehash of a previously published story. You will need a new angle, a new twist, or a new direction.

All this detective work sounds like just what it is: tedious, detailed, and hard. As a result, many writers tend to skip this step, seeing no good reason to spend so much time on research.

An analogy may help explain the necessity of such work. Finding a publisher for your short story is like job hunting (remember that for some people, writing is a full-time job). On the one hand, it seems likely that the more experience your resume reflects, the more likely a candidate you are for the job (i.e., the more publishing credits you have to your name, the more likely your work will be accepted). After all, an editor, who is often deluged with unsolicited manuscripts, may prefer manuscripts from previously published writers. Fortunately, writers can build strong resumes by publishing in local (albeit usually non-paying) markets and thereby developing impressive credentials.

On the other hand, without some detective work about the job and its responsibilities (i.e., the publication and its editorial needs), your chances of having your short story published in any given market are significantly reduced—regardless of how impressive your resume is. In other words, if you aren't right for the job, the resume makes no difference. And if your story isn't right for the publication, its quality makes no difference. So don't ignore the detective work. It is tedious, but it is essential.

PREPARING THE MANUSCRIPT

Let's assume now that you have a finished story and that you have found what seems to be the perfect publication for it. How do you prepare the manuscript?

Some general guidelines apply:

1. Use pica type, not elite, on either a typewriter or printer. (Some editors now prefer both a printed manuscript and a computer disc.)
2. Avoid novelty or decorative typefaces.
3. Avoid using a dot-matrix printer of less than 24-pin letter-quality.
4. If you do not have a laser printer, use a new black ribbon in your typewriter or printer. Avoid other ribbon colors, such as blue or green.
5. Use good paper: 16- to 20-pound bond with at least 25% rag content.
6. Avoid erasable bond—it smears.
7. Do not use a title page.
8. On the first page, place your name and address in the upper left corner, single spaced, one inch from the top of the page, 1½" from the left edge.
9. Enter the word count, rounded to the nearest 100, three spaces below your address and 1½" from the right edge.
10. Center the title one-third down the page.
11. Center "by" and your name two spaces below the title.
12. Begin the story two double spaces below your name.
13. Indent 5 spaces for new paragraphs.
14. Double-space the entire manuscript.
15. For successive pages, leave 1½" margins at the top and 1¼" margins on the other three sides.
16. Place your last name and the key words of the title on the first line at the *left* margin of every successive page. Enter the page number on the first line at the *right* margin. Skip three or four lines and begin the text.
17. After the final line of manuscript, skip two double spaces and center the words "The End."

MAILING THE MANUSCRIPT

Take the time to present your manuscript well. True, the manuscript must speak for itself, but the manner in which it arrives at an editor's desk speaks volumes before the manuscript is in hand. Here are a few guidelines:

1. Make a copy of the completed manuscript. Put the copy in your file and mail the original.
2. Mail the original manuscript addressed *by name* to the appropriate editor.

Note that a larger magazine has a special fiction editor. If the editor's name does not appear in the magazine itself (on the masthead page) or in a reference like *Writer's Market*, go to the extra time and expense of calling the switchboard and asking for the name of the person responsible for fiction. Get the correct spelling of his or her name and an accurate title (such as "assistant editor," "fiction editor," or "co-editor"). Personally addressed mail is not only more likely to reach the right desk but will also impress the editor.

3. Enclose the manuscript in a 9½" x 12½" manila mailing envelope.
4. Do not fold, staple, or paper-clip the manuscript.
5. Do not include a cover letter. The manuscript must speak for itself.
6. Enclose with the manuscript a 9" x 12" self-addressed, stamped envelope (SASE) so that the editor will return your manuscript if he or she does not purchase it.
7. If you wish, enclose a self-addressed, stamped postcard which the editor may mail to you when the manuscript is opened. You will know then that your short story is in the hands of a reader.
8. Affix adequate postage. Unless you have a postage scale, you will need to take the envelope to the post office to assure that you have adequate postage. No editor will pay postage due on a manuscript.

WAITING FOR A RESPONSE

After you have mailed the manuscript, don't waste time. Make some assumptions. If you are an optimist, assume that the story will sell its first time out. You will then be a published writer with a foot in the door for future sales. So get started on the next story. As a result of your just-completed market analysis, you may have found a publication that seems to be a perfect match with your writing style and audience appeal. If you can target such a potential market, you can tailor a story for it. Write accordingly.

If you are more pessimistic (or, some would say, more realistic), assume that your story will not sell its first time out. Begin searching immediately for the next potential market, repeating your magazine analysis, perhaps reworking the story and tailoring it for the next editor.

It's a cliché that keeping busy makes the time go faster, but the advice is worth following. Editors take from four weeks to four months to respond to an unsolicited manuscript. That's a lot of daily trips to the mailbox. Since virtually every writer faces the same frustration, however, you may as well prepare yourself for the duration. Keep busy.

If after four months you have heard nothing, write a follow-up note, detailing the submission date and the title of the story, and asking for an update on the manuscript's status. Sometimes that only seems to speed up a rejection letter, but at least you can then send your story on to the next prospective market.

HAVING YOUR MANUSCRIPT ACCEPTED

After a potentially long wait, the day comes when the mail brings an envelope from the publishing house. The editor loves your material and plans to publish it in an upcoming issue (sometimes at an unspecified time, sometimes just "within the next year"). He or she tells you what the payment will be and may occasionally include a formal contract.

Payment can range from a few complimentary copies of the magazine in which your story is printed, to a flat rate of perhaps 1½ cents a word, or to a single fee of anything from $20 to $2000. In general, you take what is offered. The alternative is to withdraw your submission, for unless you have sold regularly, you have no clout for negotiating. On the other hand, if you withdraw your submission because of a disagreement over pay, don't bother to submit there again. You should know from your detective work what pay to expect. Of course, if you are offered less than the range advertised in references like *Writer's Market*, you should question the editor about the amount and also notify the reference's publishers of the discrepancy. These publishers want their information to be accurate and will take up your complaint with the publisher—not in your behalf but in behalf of their reference work.

Pay attention, too, to the time frame for payment. Some houses pay on publication; others pay on acceptance. Thus, if the house pays on publication and the editor suggests publication "within the next year," it could be a year or more before you have cash in hand.

When you become widely known, you can negotiate not only fees but also pay dates.

CONSIDERING VANITY PRESSES

Some writers are so desperate to see their works in print that they agree to pay all or part of the expenses for having the material published. While these so-called vanity presses usually publish novels or long works of nonfiction, they have been known to gather a series of short stories by one or multiple writers and propose an anthology, paid for, of course, by each of the contributing writers.

Many of the vanity presses are reputable and do what they say they will do, but read the fine print before you get involved. Rarely do the writers get a return on their investment—and the vanity presses make no promise of such. If, nevertheless, you are willing to pay to see your work in print, go into the project with your eyes open.

DEALING WITH REJECTION

Every writer faces rejection. It is a fact of the writing life. Even very successful writers make jokes about papering their office walls— or bathroom walls—with rejection letters. On the other hand, there are rejection letters and there are rejection letters. Consider the following:

—Your manuscript is returned with a form letter addressed to "Dear Author" with two sentences: "Thank you for submitting your manuscript to Blank Magazine. Unfortunately, the work does not meet our editorial needs." It may be "signed" by "The Editors."

To get such an impersonal note after you have worked so carefully on a submission can be heartbreaking. Unfortunately, this is the most common rejection format, the one that writers refer to as "rejection forms" or "rejection slips." All of us have had our share of them. Remember, however, that the message, blunt as it is, says your story is wrong for the market. There are other markets. No one said your story is bad; the rejection slip only says your story is bad *for this market.*

Consider another scenario:

—Your manuscript is returned with the same form letter, but the editor has scribbled a personal note: "Try us again," or "This work has merit but is wrong for us."

Those brief words are exciting! The editor likes the work—your style, your approach, maybe your characters or theme—but realizes that it is inappropriate for this particular publication. The suggestion that you "try us again" is sincere and means that with a different story or slant, you'd have a chance with this editor.

Or consider yet another scenario:

—Your manuscript is returned with a rejection form and a copy of the publication's writer's guidelines and/or market requirements.

The editor is telling you that you have not followed the guidelines or met the market requirements necessary for publication in that magazine. Study both. If you can revise to meet both (and that probably means considerable revision), consider resubmitting. If not, learn your lesson: ask for guidelines and study the market requirements more carefully before you submit. You will save time (yours and the editor's) as well as postage.

Or perhaps you find yourself in yet another situation:

—You get a standard rejection form from the editor, but your manuscript is not returned.

Did you forget to send a self-addressed stamped envelope in which the editor could return your manuscript? Editors cannot provide envelopes and postage to return the hundreds—even thousands—of manuscripts they get each year. If you want yours back, you must stand the expense. If you did, in fact, send an SASE, drop the editor a note requesting the return of your manuscript, clarifying that you did indeed enclose a SASE with the manuscript (but include another SASE in case the first was lost).

Finally, you may be fortunate enough to experience one other scenario:

—Your manuscript is returned with a personal letter from the editor. The letter offers specific suggestions either for revision or for another market.

Consider yourself blessed! To have an editor take the time to personally respond is to have a little bit of heaven passed your way. Take the advice to heart. If the advice is to make revisions and you are willing to make them (and if the editor leaves the door open for a resubmission), do it! You have found an editor looking for new talent to develop, so work with him/her to develop not only your talent but also a writer–editor relationship. It can blossom into great things.

If the advice is to submit to another market, do it! An editor in one publishing house often knows what another editor is seeking. If the manuscript is wrong for his or her own publication, the editor has nothing to lose by recommending you to an editor-friend elsewhere.

THINKING POSITIVELY

Facing rejection is part of the writing business. Success is supposed to be the result of the perfect match between a publication and a writer's style and story idea. Sometimes it is also the result of a perfect match between an editor and a writer. On the other hand, sometimes it's the luck of the draw. Large publishing houses often employ "readers," usually young, aspiring editors who skim the piles of unsolicited manuscripts looking for the handful of stories that will go to the editor for final acceptance or rejection. The editor may never see your manuscript, no matter how wonderful it may be. You see, readers (and editors, too, for that matter) are only human. They have headaches, fights with their spouses, indigestion from too much pastrami at lunch. If your reader notes that he has seven minutes before he must be on his way in order to catch the 5:10 train home, your manuscript may get a very quick read before it and the standard rejection slip are shoved back into the return envelope. So, indeed, your success can be the luck of the draw—who reads your manuscript on what day and in what frame of mind. That's why you can't let rejection get you down.

On those days when you feel you have had your fill of these rejection slips, think about Madeline L'Engle, that wonderful fiction writer for children and young adults. For one of her books, she prepared a list of about twenty potential markets and methodically worked her way through the list, submitting her manuscript to first one and then another and then another. Every one rejected her work. Convinced that she had chosen the right potential markets, she simply started resubmitting. On the second trip through the list her manuscript reached the right reader. The work was published, won national acclaim, and earned her numerous interviews about her creativity. The story of her "list of twenty" made the news, and publishers wrote to her expressing their disappointment that she had not submitted her work to them. She found great pleasure in stapling a copy of their respective rejection letters to their inquiries and sending the correspondence back to haunt the editors in their dreams.

So keep the rejection slips and letters on file. You may need them! For with work, you too will find the right reader on the right day with the right publication who realizes that you are the right author with the right short story for their market. Then you can join the ranks of published writers who are ready for the *next* market!

Glossary

active voice refers to the verb whose subject is doing the acting. **Example:** Sheila ate an apple with her lunch. (*Ate* is in active voice; the subject *Sheila* is acting.) Also see *passive voice*.

adjective 1. a word that modifies nouns or pronouns. 2. a group of words functioning as an adjective, notably prepositional, participial, or infinitive phrases, or adjective clauses. **Examples:** Students *who work hard* succeed. (The adjective clause *who work hard* functions as an adjective to modify the noun *students*.) Students *standing in the hallway* waited impatiently to register. (The participial phrase *standing in the hallway* functions as an adjective to modify the noun *students*.)

adverb 1. a word that modifies a verb, adjective, or adverb. 2. a group of words functioning as an adverb, notably prepositional, participial, or infinitive phrases, or adverb clauses. **Examples:** *After our team won the game*, we celebrated. (The adverb clause modifies the verb *celebrated*.) We walked *to stay awake*. (The infinitive phrase functions as an adverb to modify the verb *walked*.)

alliteration repetition of a beginning sound, usually of a consonant, in two or more words of a phrase, line of poetry, etc. **Example:** *f*ull *f*athom *f*ive thy *f*ather lies.

antagonist a person who opposes or competes with another. Compare with *protagonist*.

assonance 1. likeness of sound, especially of vowels, as in a series of words or syllables. 2. a partial rhyme in which the stressed vowel sounds are alike but the consonant sounds are not, as in *late* and *make*.

character sketch a description of a character's most outstanding characteristics.

chronological order an arrangement in the order in which events occur.

climax the decisive turning point of the action in a short story.

complex sentence a sentence with one main clause and one or more subordinate clauses. The subordinate clause(s) may be noun, adjective, or adverb. **Example:** The child who performed the intricate ballet showed great promise. (one main clause, *the child showed great promise*, and one noun clause, *who performed the intricate ballet*.) Compare with *compound* and *compound-complex* sentences.

compound-complex sentence a sentence with two or more main clauses and one or more subordinate clauses. The subordinate clause(s) may be noun, adjective, or adverb. **Example:** The child who performed the ballet showed great promise, so the choreographer gave her special attention. (two main clauses, *the child showed great promise* and *the choreographer gave her special attention*; one subordinate clause, *who performed the ballet*.) Compare with *complex* and *compound* sentences.

compound sentence a sentence with two main clauses. **Example:** Tom made a touchdown and the crowd cheered. (two main clauses: *Tom made a touchdown* and *the crowd cheered*.) Compare with *complex* and *compound-complex* sentences.

conflict the fight, struggle, disagreement, or opposition on which a plot is based.

conflict, external a fight, struggle, disagreement, or opposition with some force outside the self, as with another person or with the surroundings.

conflict, internal a fight, struggle, disagreement, or opposition within the self.

connotation any idea suggested by or associated with a word, phrase, etc., in addition to its basic or literal meaning, or denotation.

dangling modifier a modifier with no clear reference. **Example:** His heart beating fast, the car sped away. (The participial phrase *his heart beating fast* seems to modify *car* but logically cannot. Thus, it is a dangling modifier.)

denotation the basic or literal meaning; opposite of *connotation*.

dialogue a written work in the form of a conversation.

exposition writing that sets forth facts, ideas, and detailed explanations, especially at the beginning of the short story.

falling action the part of the plot following the climax, when the conflict is resolved.

flat character a minor character, one the reader sees only as a presence.

flashback the introduction into the events of a story of an episode that took place earlier.

foreshadowing a sign of something to come, a device used especially in short stories, plays, and novels.

hyperbole exaggeration used for effect, not meant literally. **Example:** He's been teaching in that school *for a hundred years*.

imagery 1. mental images, as produced by memory or imagination. 2. descriptions and figures of speech, as in the *imagery* of a poet. In writing, usually referring specifically to sensory images, i.e., those created through the five senses.

infinitive a form of the verb which expresses existence or action without reference to person, number, or tense; usually following the marker *to*. **Example:** He likes *to work*.

infinitive phrase a word group made up of an infinitive plus its object(s) and modifier(s), functioning as an adjective, adverb, or noun. **Example:** He likes *to work hard on Mondays and Fridays*. (The infinitive phrase is the noun object of the verb *likes*.)

interior monologue the words used when a character, such as in a short story, talks to himself.

irony 1. a method of humorous or sarcastic expression in which the meaning given to the words is the opposite of their usual sense. **Example:** She used *irony* when she said the stupid plan was clever. 2. an event or result opposite to what might be expected. **Example:** That the fire station burned was an *irony*.

literary devices any of the techniques writers use to add layers of meaning, like *metaphor, simile, alliteration*, etc.

main clause a clause which can stand alone; a sentence; sometimes called an *independent clause*.

metaphor a figure of speech that suggests likeness by speaking of one thing as if it were another. **Example:** Her moods are *the endless myriads of a kaleidoscope*. Compare with *simile*.

mood the prevailing spirit or feeling in a piece of writing.

narrator a person who relates a story or account.

onomatopoeia the formation of a word by imitating the sound associated with the object or action. **Example:** *chickadee* and *clang.*

parallel structure like grammatical structures used for ideas of equal rank. **Example:** *Using computers* and *assessing data bases* are almost like second nature to him. (Two gerund phrases form parallel structures, here the compound subjects of the sentence.)

participial phrase a word group made up of a participle and its object(s) and any modifier(s). **Example:** The boy *wearing a baseball cap* must learn to take it off when entering a building. (The participle *wearing* includes an object, *cap,* and a modifier, *baseball.*)

passive voice the voice or form of a verb whose subject is the receiver (object) of the action of the verb. Generally considered a weak form. **Example:** I *was hit* by the ball. Compare with *active voice.*

personification a figure of speech in which a thing or idea is represented as a person. **Example:** The sunshine *brushed my face with a warm hand.*

plot the plan of action of a short story.

plot outline in a short story, a list of the incidents which make up the story line and lead to the author's theme.

point of view the place from which, or way in which, something is viewed; standpoint.

prepositional phrase a word group formed by a preposition and its object(s) and any modifier(s); functions as an adjective or adverb. **Example:** She supervised children *on the playground.* (functions as an adjective modifying the noun *children*)

protagonist the main character in a drama, novel, or story, around whom the action centers. Compare with *antagonist.*

resolution the part of the short story in which the plot is explained or made clear; the conclusion.

rising action in a short story, the building action which occurs from the beginning until the climax.

round character a fully-developed major character, one the reader sees as a complete person.

setting the time, place, and environment of a short story.

simile a figure of speech in which one thing is compared to another, using the word *like* or *as*. **Example:** His muscles were *as loose as last year's slingshot.* See *metaphor.*

simple sentence a single main clause without any subordinate clauses. **Example:** The boy in the red shirt won the race without difficulty.

subordinate clause a clause which cannot stand alone and depends on a main clause for its meaning; also called *dependent* clause. **Example:** The man *who came to dinner* is Dad's boss.

suspense the growing interest and excitement felt while awaiting a climax or resolution, as of a short story.

symbol a thing that stands for another thing; especially an object that stands for an idea, quality, etc. **Example:** Is the senator a *dove* or a *hawk?*

theme, implied the subject which the readers of a short story infer from the plot.

theme, stated the subject which the author states in a short story.

tone a way of wording or expressing things that shows a certain attitude.

transition a word, phrase, or sentence which connects one idea with another either within or between paragraphs.

"HOW TO" GUIDES

How to Interpret Poetry

How to Read and Write About Fiction

How to Write Book Reports

How to Write Poetry

How to Write Research Papers

How To Write Short Stories

How to Write Themes and Essays

How to Write a Thesis

AVAILABLE AT BOOKSTORES EVERYWHERE

MACMILLAN • USA